Great Prayers of the Bible

Discipleship Lessons in Petition and Intercession

by Dr. Ralph F. Wilson
Director, Joyful Heart Renewal Ministries

JesusWalk® Bible Study Series

Additional books, and reprint licenses are available at:
www.jesuswalk.com/books/greatprayers.htm

Free Participant Guide handout sheets are available at:
www.jesuswalk.com/greatprayers/greatprayers-lesson-handouts.pdf

JesusWalk® Publications
Loomis, California

Paperback

ISBN-13: 978-0-9832310-9-7

ISBN-10: 0983231095

Library of Congress Control Number: 2011916336

Library of Congress subject headings:

> Prayer – Biblical teaching
> Intercessory prayer – Christianity
> Bible – Prayers – History and criticism

Suggested Classifications

> Dewey Decimal System: 248
> Library of Congress: BV228

Published by JesusWalk® Publications, P.O. Box 565, Loomis, CA 95650-0565, USA.

JesusWalk is a registered trademark and Joyful Heart is a trademark of Joyful Heart Renewal Ministries.

Unless otherwise noted, all the Bible verses quoted are from the New International Version (International Bible Society, 1973, 1978), used by permission. Some chapters have been adapted from other books by Ralph F. Wilson. The chapter on the Lord's Prayer was adapted from Sermon on the Mount: Manifesto of the Kingdom (JesusWalk Publications, 2004). Abraham's prayer of intercession is adapted from *The Faith of Abraham* (JesusWalk, 2004). Jesus' prayer of submission in Gethsemane is adapted from *JesusWalk: Discipleship Lessons from Luke's Gospel* (2004, 2010).

110813

Preface

Rembrandt (1606-1669), "St. Jerome at Prayer" (1635), etching, 4-1/2"x3-1/8".

If you're like many believers, you long to learn to pray better, to shake off your dullness of spirit and encounter God more intimately. You want to pray with the courage of Abraham and the passion of Moses, but you're just not there yet.

There are many examples in the Bible of men and women who prayed fervent, effective prayers that God answered. That's the question: What kinds of prayers does God answer? What kind of faith does God respond to?

This book examines in considerable depth eleven profound prayers. Some are short, others lengthy. But each has something important to teach us.

The aim of this study is to help you develop in prayer, increase your faith, and move you into a new place with your Father in heaven.

However, this is not a course in learning to manipulating God to get your way. It is a study of who God is and how he responds to his children's petitions. Thus it will help you adopt God's own heart as you petition your Father.

As you model your prayers and your faith after the exemplars placed before you in God's holy Word, you'll gradually learn to take your place as a disciple of Jesus whose prayers move heaven and earth.

It is my prayer for you that you will learn to pray great prayers of faith in your own situation and for your own generation.

> Dr. Ralph F. Wilson
> Loomis, California
> December 3, 2005

Table of Contents

6. David's Psalm of Surrender to the Searcher (Psalm 139)

Reprint Guidelines

Copying the Handouts. In some cases, small groups or Sunday school classes would like to use these notes to study this material. That's great. An appendix provides copies of handouts designed for classes and small groups. There is no charge whatsoever to print out as many copies of the handouts as you need for participants.

All charts and notes are copyrighted and must bear the line:

"Copyright © 2011, Ralph F. Wilson. All rights reserved. Reprinted by permission."

You may not resell these notes to other groups or individuals outside your congregation. You may, however, charge people in your group enough to cover your copying costs. Free Participant Guide handout sheets are available at:

www.jesuswalk.com/greatprayers/greatprayers-lesson-handouts.pdf

Copying the book (or the majority of it) in your congregation or group, you are requested to purchase a reprint license for each book. A Reprint License, $2.50 for each copy, is available for purchase at

www.jesuswalk.com/books/greatprayers.htm

Or you may send a check to:

Dr. Ralph F. Wilson
JesusWalk Publications
PO Box 565
Loomis, CA 95650, USA

The Scripture says,

"The laborer is worthy of his hire" (Luke 10:7) and "Anyone who receives instruction in the word must share all good things with his instructor" (Galatians 6:6).

However, if you are from a third world country or an area where it is difficult to transmit money, please make a small contribution instead to help the poor in your community.

Introduction to Great Prayers of the Bible

I want to learn to pray better, more effectively, more meaningfully. So often I fall short. You may have had a similar experience. I believe that as we study together some of the great prayers in the Bible, we can learn better how to pray.

Over eleven weeks we'll be studying the prayers of Jesus, Abraham, Moses, Paul, and others. We'll join David in prayers of deep repentance and high praise. We'll observe as Hezekiah, Daniel, and Nehemiah call out to their God. As we study together, hopefully we can learn from their faith and boldness.

So what are the great prayers? Jesus uttered many short prayers to his Father that accomplished huge results. But we don't learn as much from the sentence or two that is recorded in the Bible, so I've looked for longer prayers

Annibale Carracci (Italian painter, 1560-1609), "St. Francis of Assisi" (1585-90).

that help us understanding the dynamics of the prayer better. This study is by no means comprehensive or exhaustive.

If you're just new to prayer, I'll try to introduce you to a few of the many of kinds of prayers that you find in the Bible. First, though, I want to introduce you to the helpful acronym ACTS, which helps guide us in our prayers:

A – Adoration. Praise and worship of God for who he is.

C – Confession. Confessing our sins and receiving his forgiveness.

T – Thanksgiving. Giving thanks for all God's blessings and answers to our prayers.

S – Supplication. Asking God for specific things. Petition is another word for this. When you ask God to meet someone else's needs, it is called intercession, the act of interceding.

As we study prayer together, we'll begin with Jesus' pattern prayer, The Lord's Prayer. Then we'll examine other prayers to see what pleases God about them. Often it is the attitude and faith of the prayer that we must learn to model. Many of these prayers are from the Old Testament, but don't consider them inferior for that reason. We learn much from them. Finally, we'll consider a couple of prayers from the New Testament.

As we study, our desire is to learn to pray better. Prayers that meet God's conditions. Prayers that pray according to God's will. By the time we finish, about three months from now I hope that we will have internalized some of these principles.

Prayer

Father, as we embark on this study of prayer, we humbly confess that we are novices. But we come longing to learn to know you through prayer. Teach us through your word, through the example of your saints. Teach us also by your Holy Spirit as you interpret the Word to our hearts. And guide us in our attempts to apply what we've learned in actual prayer. We rely on you to guide us and know you will. In Jesus' name we pray. Amen.

Abbreviations and References

BDAG   Walter Bauer and Frederick William Danker, *A Greek-English Lexicon of the New Testament and Other Early Christian Literature* (Third Edition; based on previous English editions by W.F. Arndt, F.W. Gingrich, and F.W. Danker; University of Chicago Press, 1957, 1979, 2000)

BDB   Francis Brown, S.R. Driver, and Charles A. Briggs, *A Hebrew and English Lexicon of the Old Testament* (Clarendon Press, 1907)

DOTP   T. Desmond Alexander and David W. Baker (editors), *Dictionary of the Old Testament: Pentateuch*, (InterVarsity Press, 2003)

ISBE   Geoffrey W. Bromiley (general editor), *The International Standard Bible Encyclopedia*, (Eerdmans, 1979-1988; fully revised from the 1915 edition)

KJV   King James Version (Authorized Version, 1611)

KB   Ludwig Koehler and Walter Baumgartner (editors), *Lexicon in Veteris Testamenti Libros* (Leiden: E.J. Brill, 1958)

Keil and Delitzsch   Carl Friedrich Keil and Franz Delitzsch, *Commentary on the Old Testament* (Eerdmans, reprinted 1976). Vol 1 (Pentateuch) was written by Carl Friedrich Keil, published in German in 1861, and translated by James Martin from German.

NIDNTT   Colin Brown (editor), *New International Dictionary of New Testament Theology* (Zondervan, 1975-1978; translated with additions and revisions from Theologisches Begriffslexikon zum Neuen Testament, Coenen, Beyreuther, and Bitenhard, editors)

NASB   New American Standard Bible (The Lockman Foundation, 1960-1988)

NIV   New International Version (International Bible Society, 1973, 1978)

NJB   New Jerusalem Bible (Darton, Longman & Todd Ltd, 1985)

NRSV   New Revised Standard Version (Division of Christian Education of the National Council of Churches of Christ, USA, 1989)

Thayer	Joseph Henry Thayer, *Greek-English Lexicon of the New Testament* (Associated Publishers and Authors, n.d., reprinted from 1889 edition)
TDNT	Gerhard Kittel and Gerhard Friedrich (editors), Geoffrey W. Bromiley (translator and editor), *Theological Dictionary of the New Testament*, (Eerdmans, 1964-1976; translated from Theologisches Wörterbuch zum Neuen Testament, ten volume edition)
TDOT	G. Johannes Botterweck and Helmer Ringgren (editors), John T. Willis (translator), *Theological Dictionary of the Old Testament*, (Eerdmans, 1975-)
TWOT	R. Laird Harris, Gleason L. Archer, Jr., and Bruce K. Waltke, (editors), *Theological Wordbook of the Old Testament* (2 volumes, Moody Press, 1980)

1. The Lord's Prayer (Matthew 6:5-15)

We read and recite the familiar Lord's Prayer. The Bible, of course, nowhere calls Jesus' prayer "The Lord's Prayer," nor is it called the "Our Father." How are we to look at it? Is it:

- An example prayer?
- A pattern prayer? or
- A prayer book prayer to be repeated?

It appears, from the context, to be a pattern prayer. Jesus has just criticized some of the abuses of prayer prevalent in his time: such as prayer "for effect" (verses 5-6, perhaps typified by the prayer of the righteous Pharisee contrasted by the tax collector's "Be merciful" prayer, Luke 18:9-14). Jesus has also contrasted righteous prayer with wordy prayers (vs. 7). He seems to be showing his disciples how to pray properly, avoiding some of

James Jacques Joseph Tissot (1836-1902), "The Lord's Prayer" (1886-96), watercolor, 21.6x26.4 cm, Brooklyn Museum, New York

the pitfalls, and including an appropriate mix of praise and petition.

Was this the only prayer the disciples were to pray? No. We have many prayers recorded by Jesus, his disciples, and the Apostle Paul. None of them has a word for word correspondence with The Lord's Prayer, but all of them follow patterns Jesus taught in this prayer.

Salutation: Our Father (6:9b)

The prayer begins by addressing God as "Our Father." Bible scholars pretty much agree that behind the Greek word *patēr*, "father", is the word `abba in Jesus' native Aramaic tongue.[1] Rather than the formal word for "father," `abba is the family word, something like the affectionate "Dad" or "Daddy" that we use in English. (See also Mark 14:36; Romans 8:15; Galatians 4:6). There is a formal word for "father," but the word apparently used here stresses the intimate family relationship. This is striking. Jesus was teaching his disciples to understand God as their Father. Though the rabbis spoke of God as the Father of the people, Jesus is teaching them to address God as their own personal Father, a new and wonderful revelation.

When you meditate on this a moment, the awe and wonder of it begins to break over you. The God who created the universe is our Father. The God who revealed himself in fire and smoke and thick clouds is our Father. "Father" is a relationship word, and to consider that we have the relationship of child to father with God himself is an awesome thought.

In Jesus' day, "father" included the concepts of care, love, responsibility, discipline, hopes and dreams for one's children, respect, authority, and blessing. In the West, fathers have nowhere near the life-long patriarchal authority that fathers have in the Middle East and Far East. Our fatherhood is but a shell of the powerful concept of "father" that Jesus communicated through this intimate word. Something of the Middle Eastern father is depicted in Jesus' parable of the Father and the Prodigal Son to illustrate the loving, searching, longing quality of our Heavenly Father (Luke 15:11-32).

Some in our generation have excised the word "Father" from their prayers on the basis that too many bad fathers have hurt too many children, and the image of father makes it hard for some to want to come to God. Resist this teaching that contradicts the express teaching and example of Jesus. As you meditate this week on the Lord's Prayer, I encourage you to reclaim for yourself the term "Father." Seek to find out in what ways he is a Father to you.

Notice that Jesus teaches us to call out to God as "our Father." Not just a self-focused "my father," but a communal "our Father." The Lord's Prayer is intended to be prayed not only privately, but especially in the community of God's people, the Church.

---

[1] Gotlob Schrenk, *pater, ktl.*, TDNT 5:984-985.

Who Art in Heaven (6:9)

Jesus then teaches us to pray to God "who art in heaven," which adds infinity to our understanding of God. Though Solomon built a temple for God, he prayed,

> "But will God really dwell on earth? The heavens, even the highest heaven, cannot contain you. How much less this temple I have built!" (1 Kings 8:27)

Yes, God is greater than his creation, but "the heavens" is a way to understand the greatness of God's dwelling. And when we reflect on God's greatness, it is easier to have faith to ask of him things that seem difficult to us.

Petition 1: That His Name Be Reverenced (6:9c)

The first petition is "hallowed be Thy name." The Greek word is *hagiazō*, which means "to treat as holy, reverence."[2] Our word "Halloween" is short for "All Hallows Eve," or "All Saints' Eve"). "Hallowed" comes from the English word "holy." Why does Jesus include the concept of "hallowed" in the "stripped down" version of his prayer? Because without it, our understanding of "Father" can be distorted.

Our understanding of "Father" could become sentimental to the point of presuming upon and taking advantage of the Father's graciousness towards us. "Hallowed" reminds us that the Father is holy, set apart from sin. That he can be both the Father of sinners and set apart from sin requires Jesus' atonement to reconcile. When we pray, though we pray with the privilege of intimacy to our "Abba, Daddy," we are never to imagine that we are buddies with God, or his equals. He is always our Father, and he is holy and exalted. Jesus teaches us to call God our Father, recognize his exalted place of dwelling, and to reverence him.

The phrase "hallowed be Thy name" may seem a little awkward to us, but in the Near East the idea of "name" stood for the person, his authority, his character, and his activity. When Jesus tells us that the Father's "name" is holy, he means that the Father's whole Person is holy. "Name" can be used as a substitute for a person himself. To paraphrase, "Father, hallowed be your name," means, "Father, may you be treated with the respect and honor that your holiness demands."

It is common for Christians, particularly Christians who come to faith later in their lives, to have a rather profane vocabulary. They may be in the habit of using God's name often, and sometimes almost as a swearword. If, when being surprised, we say "Lord!" or "Christ!" or "Jesus!" or "God!" we are using God's holy name in a profane and

---

[2] *Hagiazō*, BDAG 9-10.

common way. We are not reverencing his name, but debasing it. Disciples discipline their mouths and their hearts to reverence the Father's name.

Including "hallowed be your name" in our prayers means that we are to approach the Father, not only with familiarity, but also with reverence and respect for his greatness and holiness. He is our "Dad" but he is also Holy. And as we are learning to pray, we must not forget this.

Q1. What about our lives and words "hallows" the name of our Father? What desecrates and besmirches it? How should we "hallow" the Father when we begin to pray?
http://www.joyfulheart.com/forums/index.php?act=ST&f=83&t=342

Petitions 2 and 3: For His Kingdom and Will (6:10)

When we pray, too often we want to get on quickly to our own concerns. But in Jesus' model prayer, we first pray about the concerns of God's Kingdom and his will. This is not the petitioner's prayer so much as the disciple's prayer. This is how disciples are to learn to think and pray and act, with God's Kingdom foremost and predominant in their minds.

"Thy kingdom come...." What are we asking? We can't take this phrase or fragment without looking at the rest of the sentence, since the meaning is found in the context.

"Thy kingdom come, Thy will be done on earth as it is in heaven."

The Kingdom of God

The idea of the Kingdom of God is complex. It goes far back into the Old Testament, at least to the book of Exodus, where God reveals himself as Israel's King. He makes a covenant with them in the form of an ancient suzerain-vassal treaty, a treaty made between a great king and a subservient people (Exodus 19:3-6). The tabernacle in the wilderness is the throne room of a desert monarch. He leads them by day and night. Having no king but Yahweh is one of the unique marks of the Israelites, to the point that their clamoring for a king under Samuel's judgeship is considered a sin (1 Samuel 8).

Saul was Israel's first human king. David, born in Bethlehem, of the tribe of Judah, was the second king and becomes the archetypical king. He is promised that one of his sons will always sit upon the throne (2 Samuel 7), fulfilled ultimately in Jesus Christ.[3]

John comes proclaiming, "Repent, for the kingdom of heaven is near" (Matthew 3:2), and Jesus takes up the same message (Matthew 4:17). He sends out his disciples with the authority to do miracles and proclaim to villages, "The kingdom of God is near you" (Luke 10:9, 11). The kingdom of God comes when Jesus proclaims God's reign, and demonstrates that reign by preaching good news to the poor, freedom for the prisoners, sight for the blind, release for the oppressed, and the Jubilee Day of the Lord (Luke 4:18-19). The kingdom is here in Jesus and his disciples – and in you and me – but it will come fully and completely when Jesus returns to earth to reign over all as King and Lord (Revelation 11:15).

May Your Kingdom Come

Jesus asks us to pray that the Kingdom of God come soon. As one of the last phrases of the Book of Revelation says, "Amen. Come, Lord Jesus" (Revelation 22:20). The Kingdom will only be present fully when Christ returns, when "The kingdom of the world has become the kingdom of our Lord and of his Christ, and he will reign for ever and ever" (Revelation 11:15).

When we pray, "Your kingdom come," we are asking God to manifest the power and glory of his kingdom in us, and throughout our world. What a prayer! We are praying that Christ might reign over all. We are also asking the Father to hasten the return of Jesus Christ to this earth. Amen!

May Your Will Be Done on Earth

This petition is also a condition for prayer, that all our prayers conform first to God's will. How can we pray the kind of prayer that Jesus wants of us, and still ask for our petty desires that are so clearly contrary to God's revealed will in the Bible? Teach us to pray, Jesus, we say. Part of that teaching, surely, is to determine God's will and pray along those lines. Prayer for disciples is not to be selfish prayer, but prayer in tune with and guided by God's will.

---

[3] I cover this in greater detail in my essay "What Is the Kingdom of Heaven?" (www.jesuswalk.com/manifesto/kingdom-of-heaven.htm).

Q2. In what sense are we asking that the Father's kingdom should come? Why are we asking for the Father's will to be done here on earth? How should this prayer affect our living?
http://www.joyfulheart.com/forums/index.php?act=ST&f=83&t=343

Petition 4: For Daily Needs

The fourth petition in this prayer is for our own needs: "Give us this day our daily bread." This is a curious phrase, because in one short sentence it includes two words that are specific to the current day:

The word translated "This day" is Greek *semēron*, a fairly common word that means "today". But also in the sentence is an extremely rare word, which is usually translated "daily," the word *epiousios*. While its exact derivation is a matter that scholars love to debate, it probably means either "for today" or "for tomorrow."[4] Whichever it means, it is a prayer for the immediate and not distant future.

Bread, of course, is the staple of life. The word is often used for food generally, since bread is the most important food, and is extended here to mean, all of our needs, all those things that we need to sustain us.

Receiving from God

So, the prayer means something like, "Give us today what we need for today," and fits very well with Jesus' teaching later in the chapter,

> "Therefore do not worry about tomorrow, for tomorrow will worry about itself. Each day has enough trouble of its own" (Matthew 6:34).

The implication here is that we are to come to God with our daily needs. When we say "Give us," that doesn't mean we don't expect to work for our living, but that we recognize God as our Provider. So often in the Western world we have a regular salary that comes like clockwork, month after month, and we take our livelihood for granted. Only when we are laid off or touched by serious illness do we begin to ask daily for his provision. Jesus teaches us to learn to become dependent upon our Father, and to bring to him our daily needs – though we disciples are to put our own needs after the Father's holiness and kingdom and will.

---

[4] *Epiousios*, BDAG 376-377.

Our Strong Desire for Independence

It's strange, but we long to break free from the necessity of praying this prayer. We would like to store up enough money so that we don't have to worry – or pray – about where our next meal will come from. We would like to be "comfortably" well off, if not rich. We don't want to have to pray for our next meal.

I don't think that Jesus wants us poverty-stricken (though that may happen to us and in that he will be fully able to meet our needs). But he does want us to get in the habit of relying upon the Father – for everything. Should we thank God for our food if we have earned the money for it by our own labor? Of course!

> "You may say to yourself, 'My power and the strength of my hands have produced this wealth for me.' But remember the Lord your God, for it is he who gives you the ability to produce wealth, and so confirms his covenant, which he swore to your forefathers, as it is today." (Deuteronomy 8:17-18)

Since it is God who gives us the ability to earn a living, then in a real sense, it is he who "gives" us our daily bread. He strengthens us, and provides through us. So often, when we have our health, we take this ability for granted. Jesus is teaching us to look to the Father for every provision.

Sometimes you hear the teaching that we should pray for others' needs, but never for our own, that God will provide without us even asking. Though that teaching sounds pious and faith-filled, it goes directly counter to Jesus' own teaching. We are to ask God for our daily needs. He is interested in our jobs. He cares about your school. He is concerned about the health of your business. He cares about your marriage, and children, and relationships. Your church matters to him.

Jesus teaches us, "Give us today our daily bread." How is it that we so often confuse such a simple concept?

Q3. Why do we seek to be independent of asking *anyone* for help? Why do we seek to be independent of God? Why should we ask God to "give" us daily bread so long as we can earn a living for ourselves?
http://www.joyfulheart.com/forums/index.php?act=ST&f=83&t=344

Petition 5: Forgiveness (Matthew 6:12, 14-15)

The fifth petition is for forgiveness. But like the daily-ness of the fourth petition, the fifth petition, too, has a twist. The prayer is:

"Forgive us our debts,
   as we forgive our debtors."

Three Greek words are used in relationship to sin in The Lord's Prayer in Matthew and Luke. Christians from different traditions use different words as they recite The Lord's Prayer.

"Debt" (Matthew 6:12), Greek *opheilema*, "debt = what is owed, one's due." Here, it is used in a religious sense debt = sin (as Aramaic *hobah* in rabbinical literature).[5]

"Trespass" (Matthew 6:14-15, KJV), Greek *paraptōma*, "in imagery of one making a false step so as to lose footing: a violation of moral standards, offense, wrongdoing, sin."[6] *Paraptōma* is a compound word from *para*, "beside or near" + *piptō*, "to fall." Thayer defines it as "a lapse or deviation from truth and uprightness; a sin, misdeed."[7]

"Sin" (Luke 11:4), Greek *hamartia*, "sin. The action itself as well as its result, every departure from the way of righteousness...."[8] Literally, "a failing to hit the mark."[9]

But this prayer, "Forgive us our debts, as we forgive our debtors," is a sort of trick prayer. It is a prayer Jesus uses to teach his disciples the elements of praying aright. The Greek word *hōs*, is a conjunction marking a point of comparison, meaning "as."[10] Jesus teaches us to ask God to forgive us "as" we forgive others. In other words, if we forgive others only a little and hold grudges, we are asking God to forgive us only a little and bear a grudge against us. Wow! How many people pray the Lord's Prayer thoughtlessly, and each time they pray, they pray a curse of unforgiveness down upon themselves!

Jesus is making a point in this prayer, a point which he explains in more detail just after the prayer:

"For if you forgive men when they sin against you, your heavenly Father will also forgive you. But if you do not forgive men their sins, your Father will not forgive your sins." (Matthew 6:14-15)

How could it be plainer? Jesus had just told his disciples not to seek retribution.

"Love your enemies and pray for those who persecute you,
   that you may be sons of your Father in heaven" (Matthew 5:44-45).

Now he makes it clear that we must forgive, if we are to be considered sons of the Father. Otherwise he will not forgive us.

[5] *Opheilema*, BDAG 743.
[6] *Paraptōma*, BDAG 770.
[7] *Paraptōma*, Thayer 485.
[8] *Hamartia*, BDAG 43-44.
[9] *Hamartia*, Thayer 30.
[10] *Hōs*, BDAG 1103-1106.

It is a hard saying, but it is God's way.

Quintessential Forgiveness

Perhaps the most powerful example is that of Jesus himself. "He came to his own [people]," John records, "and his own [people] did not receive him" (John 1:12). His miracles and bread attracted the crowds, but when he had to say some hard things, they would leave as quickly as they had come (John 6:66). A number of times, when he said something they didn't consider Kosher, they tried to kill him, but he slipped away from their grasp (Luke 4:28-30; John 8:59; 10:31). But the time finally came that God had planned (Galatians 4: 4-5). Jesus knew it was coming, and though it filled him with pain to think of it, he faced it openly. This time when his enemies sought to arrest him, he stood forth, said "I am the man," and allowed them to take him. He allowed a mock trial filled with patently false and unsupported charges. He could have called legions of angels to deliver him – the armies of heaven were at his beck and call – but he did not. Soldiers spit in his face and mocked him with a cruel crown of thorns and a purple robe they said made him look like a king. They scourged him nearly to death. Pilate washed his hands and ordered his crucifixion. And as they crucified him, he said, "Father, forgive them, for they know not what they do" (Luke 23:34).

If we are to know and understand God, we must love. We must know and understand forgiveness. If we reject this part of God, we reject the kernel of who he is (1 John 4:16-21). So when Jesus puts it so bluntly in our passage (6:14-15) – you must forgive to be forgiven – we dare not reject this truth.

Isn't this a sort of "works righteousness"? some ask. If you are required to do something before you can be forgiven, then isn't this righteousness by works? No. There's an old story of how to catch a monkey. You chain a cage to a post, and put an orange in the cage. Then when the monkey tries to grasp the orange, and can't pull it through the bars he is trapped. Can't he just release the orange and escape? Yes, but monkeys don't let go of the things that enslave them. They hold on tightly – just like people. And so he is captured, just as surely as if he were in the cage itself.

To be free you must let go of unforgiveness. Is that meritorious so as to earn heaven? No, not any more than repentance from sin is meritorious. We don't earn heaven by repentance or by forgiving. But we must let go of our bondage to sin and hate if we want to receive something better.

The Struggle to Forgive

Forgiveness is sometimes terribly difficult. It's usually not so hard to forgive people we don't know. The people with whom we have a relationship of trust who turn on us, who betray our trust – those people are the hardest to forgive. Husbands, wives, fathers, mothers, children, and boyfriends and girlfriends and our best friends. They can turn on us and wound us deeply. Sometimes we even doubt that "It is better to have loved and lost, than never to have loved at all." Maybe we should withdraw and protect ourselves and never venture out again.

No. The path of health is forgiveness. The path of healing is forgiving.

Sometimes we resist forgiveness because we mistake it for substitutes. In my article "Don't Pay the Price of Counterfeit Forgiveness,"[11] I try to distinguish true forgiveness from its chameleons. True forgiveness does not minimize the sin or the hurt, nor excuse the sinner. True forgiveness chooses not to hold the sin against the sinner any longer. True forgiveness is pardon.

You may be freshly wounded and find your anger too massive to forgive. The injustice may be ongoing, the outrage constant. Perhaps you do not feel you are able to forgive right now. Then I ask you to pray this prayer: "Lord, I find it beyond my ability to forgive this person. I ask you to make me *able* to forgive in the future." Even that prayer may stretch your faith (or obedience) to pray, but pray it anyway. The God of Forgiveness answers prayers like that. He makes a way where there is no way. He takes us beyond ourselves.

Two simple lessons we disciples learn from this petition: (1) we must ask for forgiveness time and time again, and (2) unforgiveness blocks God's blessing.

Q4. Why should we continually ask forgiveness? How can unforgiveness on our part block God's blessing? How can unforgiveness block God's forgiveness?
http://www.joyfulheart.com/forums/index.php?act=ST&f=83&t=345

Petitions 6 and 7: Help When Tempted (6:13)

"And lead us not into temptation,
but deliver us from the evil one." (6:13)

---

[11] "Don't Pay the Price of Counterfeit Forgiveness" (*Moody Monthly,* October 1985, pp. 106-108 (www.joyfulheart.com/maturity/forgive.htm)

The sixth petition goes beyond asking for forgiveness; it asks for help in our times of trial and temptation so that we do not sin so as to require forgiveness.

Keep Us from Temptation

On its face it is hard to imagine God leading us into temptation at all.

> "When tempted, no one should say, 'God is tempting me.' For God cannot be tempted by evil, nor does he tempt anyone; but each one is tempted when, by his own evil desire, he is dragged away and enticed." (James 1:13-14)

Sometimes we disciples flirt with temptation. We don't exactly seek temptation, but we are attracted to sinful things and so we sort of wink at them. Our resistance is low; we are being "dragged away and enticed" by our "own evil desire," as James puts it. This prayer, "and lead us not into temptation," helps teach us how important it is for us to stop flirting with sin but to actively flee and resist it. That is to be part of the content of our prayers.

Some of you are saying, "But if God knew what I really thought about, or wanted to do, he wouldn't have anything to do with me." Some of you are ashamed of your secret sins, but afraid to open them up to God himself. My dear friends, there is nothing we have done or said or thought that can surprise our Father. The miracle of the cross is that he cares about us in spite of our rebelliousness. This part of the Lord's Prayer reminds us to call upon the Father for strength when we are tempted. We are not to fight a secret war against sin; the Father wants to be our continual partner. He knows your weakness, and mine. And wants to free us and make us whole. What a wonderful Father! What wonderful grace.

But God does *test* us. He allows circumstances that stretch and try us to make us pliable enough that he can remold us into his own image.

> "Consider it pure joy, my brothers, whenever you face trials of many kinds, because you know that the testing of your faith develops perseverance." (James 1:2-3)

Job was tested. So were Abram and Jacob and Joseph – and Jesus. Trials can be positive, and Jesus wouldn't be teaching us to pray to escape what is strengthening us. So it is probably better to see "Lead us not into temptation," as the negative of its positive counterpart, "but deliver us from evil." Testing may involve temptations, but God's desire is to help us escape temptation – and the tempter. Here we're praying: Don't lead us into places where we can be tempted, but lead us in places where you are, and where we can be free.

Rescue Us from the Evil One

This seventh petition is a prayer for deliverance or rescue from the evil one. It is recognition of the spiritual nature of our warfare against sin. There is not just our own temptation, but a tempter. In our own selves, we are no match for him. So we call out to God for rescue, for deliverance, for salvation from our enemy.

Together, petitions six and seven are asking God: "Keep us from giving into Satan's temptations."

Petition five deals with forgiveness; six and seven with delivering us from sin. Together they make up a prayer that helps us follow Jesus on his path.

A Doxology (6:13c)

"For Thine is the kingdom,
and the power,
and the glory forever.
Amen."

Having been raised a Protestant, the first time I heard the Catholic version of the Lord's Prayer that left off the last doxology, I was shocked. It was like waiting for the other shoe to drop – and it never did. Actually, the Catholic version may be closer to Jesus' own words than the Protestant version. Let me explain.

The Protestant version of the Lord's Prayer includes a doxology. Our English word "doxology" comes from two Greek words, *doxa* – "praise," and *logos* – "word"; a "word of praise." Sometimes it is called an ascription, since these qualities are "ascribed" to God.

Our best guess is that the doxology was added – perhaps on the basis of 1 Chronicles 29:11-13 – to adapt the Lord's Prayer for liturgical use in the early church. Although the doxology was probably not part of the original text, Jewish practice was to conclude prayers with a doxology, so it is unlikely that it was offered in New Testament times without some form of doxology.[12] One of my favorite parts of the Lord's Prayer is the

---

[12] The discipline of Textual Criticism tries to determine which version of a disputed text is closest to the original words that Jesus actually said. The original Gospel of Matthew was doubtless copied for use in other churches. And each of those copies became the source of yet more copies, families of copies. In the last century and a half scholars have categorized the earliest manuscripts we have into families of manuscripts according to the similarities found between them. Some of the earliest manuscript families lack the doxology – specifically Alexandrian (Aleph and B), Western (D and most of the Old Latin), and the pre-Caesarean (*f*1) types. Those that include it are K L W Delta Theta, Pi, and *f*13, *et al*. A few manuscripts (such as the *Didache* have a different doxology altogether. Some of the earliest Church Fathers (Tertullian, Origen, and Cyprian, for example) didn't include the doxology in their commentaries on the

doxology. I love to speak out loud as words of declaration and praise, "For Thine is the Kingdom, and the Power, and the Glory," for all these are his in abundance. Praise is a fitting way to conclude our prayer.

The Disciples' Prayer

The Lord's Prayer is deceptively simple. We may pray it often and by rote. We may take its words for granted. But this week – especially this week – let the prayer that Jesus taught his disciples to pray fill your thoughts and meditations. And may its vocabulary become yours.

As we've examined the Lord's Prayer, you can see it isn't a prayer for everyone. It's not for those who hunger for God to rubber-stamp their selfish plans, for it begins with "Thy will be done on earth as it is in heaven." Nor is it for those who feel righteous, for it leads us to ask forgiveness. Nor is it for the vindictive, for it bids us leave our hatred at the altar if we would be forgiven. Nor is it for the self-made man who shuns dependence, for it teaches us to ask God for bread daily. It is a prayer for the obedient disciple who would know God as he is, in his Fatherhood and glory and holiness. I commend it to you. Pray it thoughtfully and reverently, and let it guide your prayers.

Prayer

Father, teach me to pray the right way, the way Jesus taught us to pray. I confess that my way of praying is often self-centered and self-serving. Teach me to pray. In Jesus' name, I pray. Amen.

Key Verses

> "'Our Father in heaven, hallowed be your name,
> your kingdom come, your will be done
> on earth as it is in heaven.
> Give us today our daily bread.
> Forgive us our debts,
> as we also have forgiven our debtors.
> And lead us not into temptation,
> but deliver us from the evil one.'" (Matthew 6:9-13)

Lord's Prayer. So W.L. Liefeld, "Lord's Prayer," *ISBE* 3:162. See Bruce M. Metzger, *A Textual Commentary on the Greek New Testament* [United Bible Societies, 1971], pp. 16-17. At some point the use of the doxology had dropped out in Roman Catholic liturgy. John Calvin (1509-1564) comments, "It is surprising that this clause ... has been left out by the Latins...." (*A Commentary on a Harmony of the Evangelists, in loc.*). John A. Broadas (*Matthew*, p. 139) notes that the doxology wasn't introduced into the English *Book of Common Prayer* until the time of Charles II.

2. Moses' Intercession for Israel (Exodus 32:9-14)

"Moses Praying" (1922) by J.H. Hartley (illustrator), in James Bailie, *The Bible Story: a connected narrative retold from Holy Scripture* (A & C Black Ltd., London, 1923)

This passage is the first of two occasions where Moses intercedes for sinful Israel before an angry God who is ready to wipe them out – and succeeds in appealing for mercy for them. We'll be focusing on Exodus 32:1-10, but will allude to Numbers 14:11-24 where Israel's unbelief at entering the Promised Land also turns to rebellion.

I'm taking Moses' intercession out of chronological order in our study of prayer – before Abraham's intercession, that is – because the truths this passage teaches are so utterly radical and vital to a foundational understanding of prayer. The real issue at stake here is: Can prayer change God's mind? Or does prayer affect only us who pray?

Setting the Scene

Moses has been on Mt Sinai with God for forty days and nights receiving from God the terms of the Covenant and overview of the Tabernacle, setting up for Israel the Kingdom under God as King. Finally, the finger of God inscribes the Ten Commandments on two stone tablets.

But while Moses is there before God, the people on the sands below have become impatient. They demand that Aaron make visible gods like they're used to. From their gold earrings Aaron fashions a gold calf. In spite of Aaron's feeble efforts to try to turn this into a festival to Yahweh, the people worship the golden calf idol, sacrifice to it, and claim that the idol brought them out of Egypt – utter blasphemy. Where we pick up the story, God is utterly disgusted and filled with anger – very righteous anger to be sure! He says:

> "'I have seen these people,' the LORD said to Moses, 'and they are a stiff-necked people. Now leave me alone so that my anger may burn against them and that I may destroy them. Then I will make you into a great nation.'" (Exodus 32:9-10)

"Stiff-necked" is a reference to a mule or ox that would resist the lead rope and refuse to let its master lead it. Instead, it would stiffen its neck against the reins.

Embarrassment at an Angry God

The people have utterly rebelled against God by substituting idols and attributing God's salvation to them. This is treason against the Monarch. This is rebellion.

God is angry – "wroth," you might say. Cole calls this "a deliberate 'anthropopath-ism,' [*anthropos* mankind + *pathos* feelings, passion] describing God's feelings in human terms, as being more comprehensible to us."[1] "Now, now...," some people might chide God. "You shouldn't be angry. Anger is an emotion that can get you in trouble, God. Cool down. Be calm and serene." Yeah, right! Is that the way you act when you are challenged? Of course not! God gave us the emotion of anger so that we might act in the face of unrighteousness and challenge rather than remain passive. It is a defense mechanism that we need for survival.

God's anger at sin can't be understood apart from his own holiness, his separateness from sin, his nature utterly opposed to injustice, sin, and human degradation. Our sins offend God's very character. The Bible contains hundreds of statements of God's anger at sin. We, too, are told, "Let those who love the LORD hate evil" (Psalm 97:10a).

If you can't accept an angry God, then you won't be able to understand him. If God's anger at sin offends you, then you have placed yourself above God as his judge, with no understanding of God's holiness or his mercy. Is God's anger merely an anthropomor-phism, a solely human attribute projected upon God? I don't think so. That's too easy a dismissal of a characteristic of God which is enmeshed in our entire revelation of him and his character.

---

[1] R. Alan Cole, *Exodus* (Tyndale Old Testament Commentaries; Inter-Varsity Press, 1973), p. 216.

God's Judgment on Israel (32:10)

God tells Moses that he will destroy the nation of Israel, and reconstruct the nation from Moses' own offspring. Since Moses himself is a direct descendent of Abraham, Isaac, and Jacob, God's promises to the patriarchs would be fulfilled. God had destroyed mankind once and restarted it with Noah and his descendents (Genesis 6-8); Moses has every reason to believe that God is quite serious.

Q1. Read Exodus 32:1-14. What had the people done that was so bad? How can a loving God be angry? Is God's sentence to destroy Israel and raise up a new nation through Moses justified?
http://www.joyfulheart.com/forums/index.php?act=ST&f=84&t=346

Elements of Moses' Intercession (32:11-13)

Moses' intercession is a clear example of someone who has taken God's interests into his heart as his own. Even though in a way Moses' own family would benefit from God's proposal as the New Patriarchs, Moses appeals to God, boldly interceding for the people of Israel, pleading for mercy rather than condemnation upon them. And in the end God relents and responds positively to Moses' prayer. We'll consider the theological implications of this shortly. But first I want to analyze Moses' argument before God. Since the prayers in Exodus 32 and Numbers 14 are similar, I'm showing them together so you can compare them.

Exodus 32:11-13

Appeal that the people of Israel are God's own people. "O LORD," he said, "why should your anger burn against *your people*, whom you brought out of Egypt with great power and a mighty hand?"

Appeal to God's name and reputation. "Why should the Egyptians say, 'It was *with evil intent* that he brought them out, to kill them in the mountains and to wipe them off the face of the earth'"?

Basic prayer. "Turn (*šub*) from your fierce anger; relent (*nācham*) and do not bring disaster on your people.

Appeal to God's promises to the patriarchs. "Remember your servants *Abraham, Isaac and Israel*, to whom you swore by your own self: 'I will make your descendants as numerous as the stars in the sky and I will give your descendants all this land I promised them, and it will be their inheritance forever.'" (Exodus 32:11-13)

Numbers 14:13-19

Appeal to God's reputation. "Then the Egyptians will hear about it! By your power you brought these people up from among them. And they will tell the inhabitants of this land about it. They have already heard that you, O LORD, are with these people and that you, O LORD, have been seen face to face, that your cloud stays over them, and that you go before them in a pillar of cloud by day and a pillar of fire by night. If you put these people to death all at one time, the nations who have heard this report about you will say, 'The LORD was not able to bring these people into the land he promised them on oath; so he slaughtered them in the desert.'"

Appeal to God's character of mercy. "Now may the LORD's strength be displayed, just as you have declared: 'The LORD is slow to anger, abounding in love and forgiving sin and rebellion. Yet he does not leave the guilty unpunished; he punishes the children for the sin of the fathers to the third and fourth generation.' In accordance with your great love, forgive the sin of these people...."

Appeal to God's precedent. "... Just as you have pardoned them from the time they left Egypt until now." (Numbers 14:13-19)

When I read Moses' intercession it makes me think of a Prime Minister appealing to the King to alter his decree so that it is in keeping with the concerns of foreign relations, previous treaties, the King's character, and previous decrees. Notice the basis of Moses' appeals:

- Because the Israelites are God's own people
- Because of God's reputation among the heathen
- Because of God's promises
- Because of God's character
- Because of God's consistent mercy.

As we study the great prayers of the Bible, we begin to see a pattern where intercessors state their case before God based on his promises, character, righteousness, and precedents. When we learn to pray this way, we begin to learn to pray according to the will of God rather than contrary to it. When we support our prayers with appeals to scripture, we align ourselves with God's will. Part of learning to pray is praying scripture back to God.

Q2. What aspects of Moses' prayer of intercession should we emulate in our own prayers? Upon what logical grounds does Moses offer this bold appeal to God? What do you think it means to "pray the promises of God"? How does knowing the Bible help you get your prayers answered? How does this help our prayers be within God's will?

http://www.joyfulheart.com/forums/index.php?act=ST&f=84&t=347

Moses' bold prayer and God's positive response raise all sorts of questions about the nature of prayer. What is it? Why is it? What prayers will God answer?

Can Prayer Affect the Outcome of God's Actions?

You'll find a number of writers that seem to imply that prayer doesn't change God, it changes us. While, no doubt, the process of prayer does change us, nevertheless Exodus 32 clearly indicates that Moses' prayer changed God's proposed actions. If this is true, then prayer is powerful, since by prayer we can appeal to and induce God to do something he otherwise would not have done. That's the basic premise that underlies a prayer of petition or intercession.

Predestination and Prayer

Some branches of Christianity have a strong deterministic bent. "*Que sera, sera,* What will be, will be." There is no changing it. God has both foreknown and determined all things from all eternity. Everything is fixed. It is now all playing out as some kind of cosmic automate chess game where the pieces move as they are programmed and each move is a foregone conclusion. I may be overplaying this to make a point, but it does represent one approach to prayer.

If it is true that our prayers can cause a change in the outcome that God brings to pass, how does this relate to predestination? Let me simplify an impossibly complex subject for a moment, realizing that not all will agree with my definitions. (Theologians have argued about these unknowable things for many centuries.[2])

---

[2] You'll find a recent and fair discussion of predestination, free will, Calvinism, and Arminianism in Wayne Grudem, *Systematic Theology* (Zondervan, 1994, ISBN 0310286700). Grudem takes a reformed position, though is sympathetic to several Arminian arguments.

- **Predestination**. The belief that God foreordains, predestines, or predetermines whatsoever shall happen in history. That is, God causes to come to pass every-thing that happens. (Some would deny that God wills sinful actions.)
- **Foreknowledge**. The belief that God knows about everything that will take place before it happens (thus presupposing that the end of all things is fixed).
- **Free will**. The belief that human beings are given a real freedom to make choices, free of compulsion, if not free of influence.

Most Christians I know say they believe in foreknowledge – the very nature of prophecy requires foreknowledge. But I've heard many Christians say somewhat proudly that they don't believe in predestination, though the Bible clearly teaches it as well (for example: Proverbs 16:4; Acts 1:7; 2:23; 4:28; Romans 8:29-30; 9:11; Ephesians 1:4-5, 9-11; 3:11; 1 Peter 1:2, 20). Most Christians, especially Americans, believe in free will; it would be undemocratic not to believe in it.

How do you fit together predestination and free will? Frankly, I don't fully know, though I know that the Bible affirms both God's sovereignty and our responsibility to act righteously.

The reason I even bring up the subject of predestination is because our passage raises serious problems to Christians who believe that everything set, fixed, immutable, predetermined – signed, sealed, and delivered.

For example, C.F. Keil writes:

> "God puts the fate of the nation into the hand of Moses, that he may remember his mediatorial office and show himself worthy of his calling."

Then he asks what would have happened if Moses' had failed the test. He concludes:

> "The possibility of such a thing, however, is altogether an abstract thought: the case supposed could not possibly have occurred, since God knows the hearts of His servants, and foresees what they will do, though, notwithstanding His omniscience, He gives to human freedom room enough for self-determination, that He may test the fidelity of His servants. No human speculation, however, can fully explain the conflict between divine providence and human freedom."[3]

Keil is acknowledging that Moses' prayer changed God's action, but then seems compelled to hedge Moses' prayer around with predestination so that it couldn't have been any other way. I know we really don't understand predestination, no matter how

---

[3] C.F. Keil, "The Second Book of Moses," in C.F. Keil and F. Delitzsch, *Commentary on the Old Testament in Ten Volumes* (Eerdmans, reprinted 1976).

much we might argue for or against it. But what we *must* understand is that Moses' prayer – and your prayers – can affect God's action.

When it comes to you and your prayers, you must act as if everything is *not* predetermined. You must believe that your prayers can change God's mind and action. If you don't, you won't be able to pray like Moses or Abraham or Elijah, but only a passive, "Thy will be done." Certainly, Jesus prayed that prayer, but only after wrestling in prayer with his Father. Our problem is that we are unwilling to wrestle in prayer as did Moses. We don't believe in the power of prayer, so we pray wimpy prayers.

Many centuries after Moses, James tells us: "The effectual fervent prayer of a righteous man availeth much" (KJV, James 5:16b) or "The prayer of a righteous man is powerful and effective" (NIV). Either we believe it and will act on it, or we are passive and unbelieving in our prayers.

Q3. How can a wrong understanding of determinism and predestination keep us from the kind of gutsy prayer that Moses prayed? What do you call a belief that our prayers make no difference to God's response?
http://www.joyfulheart.com/forums/index.php?act=ST&f=84&t=348

Inviting Intercession (Exodus 32:10)

The real question here is how does God want us to pray? Look carefully at verse 10:

"Now leave me alone so that my anger may burn against them and that I may destroy them. Then I will make you into a great nation." (Exodus 32:10)

It's almost as if the LORD is inviting Moses to intercede for the nation, as if he were to say, "*If* you do not let me alone (i.e., intercede), *then* I will destroy them...." God could have shut the door as he did in Deuteronomy 3:26 when Moses requests permission to enter the promised land, but God doesn't.[4]

Again and again in the Bible we see men and women of God wrestling in prayer with God until they receive the answer they seek. By their examples littering the pages of the Book, I conclude that God wants us to pray with the same faith, fervency, and fortitude.

[4] Brevard S. Childs, *The Book of Exodus* (The Old Testament Library; Westminster Press, 1974).

Repenting or Relenting (Exodus 32:14)

Besides predestination, theologians have trouble with prayer and the Doctrine of Immutability, that is, that God is unchanging in nature, desire, and purpose. Since our passage insists that prayer somehow changes God's mind, we may balk at believing this. Key to our understanding of prayer is verse 14:

> "Then the LORD relented and did not bring on his people the disaster he had threatened." (Exodus 32:14)

The word translated "relented" (NIV), "repented" (KJV), and "changed his mind" (NRSV) is the Hebrew verb *nācham*, "be sorry, repeat, regret, be comforted, comfort." In the majority of cases, this verb refers to God's repentance, not man's. When man's repentance is in view, the Hebrew verb *shub* is mainly used.[5]

Man repents from sin towards God; God is free from sin. So when God repents or relents it is a decision to change his action without any notion of wrongdoing or sin. While some verses that use *nācham* seem to indicate God's changing his mind on an arbitrary basis, in many places it is clear that the change is due to changed circumstances. A. J. Heschel has said,

> "No word is God's final word. Judgment, far from being absolute, is conditional. A change in man's conduct brings about a change in God's judgment."[6]

See, for example, 1 Samuel 15:29 with 1 Samuel 15:11. The classic passage is in the analogy of the potter and the clay, where the LORD explains to Jeremiah:

> "If at any time I announce that a nation or kingdom is to be uprooted, torn down and destroyed, and if that nation I warned repents (*shub*) of its evil, then I will relent (*nācham*) and not inflict on it the disaster I had planned. And if at another time I announce that a nation or kingdom is to be built up and planted, and if it does evil in my sight and does not obey me, then I will reconsider (*nācham*) the good I had intended to do for it." (Jeremiah 18:7-10)

God's character, holiness, and purpose do not change. Cole observes, "In the Bible, it is clear that God's promises and warnings are always conditional on man's response," as in Ezekiel 33:13-16.[7] One of those responses is prayer and intercession.

---

[5] Marvin R. Wilson, *nācham*, TWOT #1344.
[6] Abraham Herschel, *The Prophets*, p. 194, cited in TWOT #1344.
[7] Cole, *Exodus*, p. 17. Also J.R. Soza, "Repentance," DOTP 684-687.

Immutability and the Will of God

Victor Hamilton concludes,

> "The fact that the Old Testament affirms that God does repent, even over a *fait accompli* [accomplished fact] forces us to make room in our theology for the concepts of both the unchangeability of God and his changeability."[8]

The doctrine of God's immutability does not restrict God's action. It means that God's character, desire, and purpose do not change.

When you carry a strong deterministic bent down to the minute by minute level, then God has an opinion about whether you brush your teeth at 9 pm rather than 10 pm. Or your brand of toothpaste. You should seek God's will about whether or not to wash your hands two times during an afternoon or three. I see this as way overdone.

I agree with the immutability of God, that his character, desire, and purpose do not change. But I see it as more dynamic and adjustable – though strong predestinarians will doubtless disagree. If a rocket's destination is the moon, then the onboard computer is constantly making tiny corrections to ensure that the rocket ultimately gets to the moon, even though its trajectory might have varied a bit from the ideal plotted by astrophysicists at the Jet Propulsion Lab. A river may be broad, but there are definite banks which determine how widely it can flow. I see God's will as boundaries within which we are free to live and pray.

In Moses' case, both alternatives were within God's will:

1.   Destroying Israel and raising up a new nation through Moses, *and*

2.   Preserving and pardoning the nation while chastising it.

Moses didn't ask God to do something that was clearly out of his will, but to select another choice which was entirely consistent with God's revealed will and character. In Moses' mind, Plan B was preferable to Plan A, and he argued eloquently before God for Plan B.

We are commanded in Hebrews:

> "Let us therefore come boldly unto the throne of grace, that we may obtain mercy, and find grace to help in time of need" (Hebrews 4:16)

---

[8] Victor P. Hamilton, *The Book of Genesis: Chapters 1-17* (New International Commentary on the Old Testament; Eerdmans, 1990), p. 275, commenting on God regretting creating mankind in Genesis 6:6.

Q4. How can prayer change God's mind without conflicting with the doctrine of the Immutability of God? Can God answer a prayer for something outside of the scope of his will?
http://www.joyfulheart.com/forums/index.php?act=ST&f=84&t=349

Having the Family Business at Heart

Was God pleased with Moses? Oh, yes! Because Moses had learned to pray with God's kingdom at heart. Moses' prayer was guided by references to God's character, God's reputation, God's precedents, God's best interests. What a joy for God to hear that prayer! No wonder he answered Moses positively.

What is God doing in teaching us to pray? He is seeking raise a generation of sons and daughters who have in their heart the good of the family business – that is, the Kingdom of God. When we learn to pray like Moses, we no longer seek our own good, but God's good, God's interests, God's kingdom. By prayer we grapple with the issues that affect the

Kingdom here on earth. As we pray our minds are aligned with his will and our petitions and our intercessions are met with clear answers.

So does prayer change God or change us? Both. As we learn to pray like Moses we learn to pray according to God's will. We are changed. But as we pray according to God's will, God is willing to change his actions to respond to our intercessions and petitions. We are after all his children and he is our Father. Jesus taught us:

> "Which of you, if his son asks for bread, will give him a stone? Or if he asks for a fish, will give him a snake? If you, then, though you are evil, know how to give good gifts to your children, how much more will your Father in heaven give good gifts to those who ask him!" (Matthew 7:9-11)

In prayer, our Father invites us to ask us what is on our hearts – our changed hearts – and he delights to answer us. Why pray? Because your prayers affect the way your Father, the Sovereign of the Universe, will conduct his affairs. Prayer is truly awesome!

Prayer

Father, forgive me. So often I act as if prayer isn't really that important. Teach me in my heart of hearts the power of prayer that I might be used by you to influence my generation for Christ. In Jesus' name, I pray. Amen.

Key Verse

"Then the LORD relented and did not bring on his people the disaster he had threatened." (Exodus 32:14)

3. Abraham's Prayer for Sodom (Genesis 18:16-33)

Abraham's prayer for Sodom – really for Lot and his family – is an amazing revelation of the faith of one man in the justice of Almighty God and an incredible boldness of a mere human before the Creator of the Universe. Abraham seems to stand before God alone, yet wields significant influence over God's actions.

Perhaps for Jewish readers, Abraham is the classic example of both Jewish chutzpah as well as a gift for bargaining. But I think he is much, much more. He has learned to pray. Let's consider the passage together.

Setting the Stage

Years before Abraham had emigrated to Canaan along with his nephew Lot, but as the uncle he retained a strong obligation to protect his nephew, a

Marc Chagall (Russian- born French painter, 1887-1985), "The Praying Jew (Rabbi of Vitebsk)" (1923, copy of 1914 work), oil on canvas, 116.8 x 89.4 cm, Art Institute of Chicago.

member of his extended family. Lot had settled in Sodom, a sinful city in the fertile valley near the Dead Sea. Once, when the kings of Mesopotamia sacked Sodom and carried off Lot and other residents as slaves, Abraham raised his own personal military force, attacked the Mesopotamian army by night, rescued Lot, and returned him to his home (Genesis 14:1-16).

But now Lot is threatened by another overpowering force – God himself. And Abraham finds himself contending for Lot before the Lord. Abraham has entertained three men. It turns out that two of them are angels on their way to Sodom and the third is Yahweh himself.

Here is where our story begins.

The Sins of Sodom and Gomorrah (Genesis 18:20-21)

> "Then the LORD said, 'The outcry against Sodom and Gomorrah is so great and their sin so grievous that I will go down and see if what they have done is as bad as the outcry that has reached me. If not, I will know.'" (Genesis 18:20-21)

"Outcry against" (NIV, NRSV) or "cry of" (KJV) is the Hebrew noun za'ārā, "cry, outcry." The basic meaning of this root is "to cry for help in time of distress."[1] A similar outcry of the oppressed for justice is heard throughout the Old Testament (Genesis 4:10; Exodus 2:23-24; 3:7, 9; 22:23, 27; Deuteronomy 24:15; Job 31:38-39; 34:28; Psalm 9:12; 10:17; 22:24; 34:6; 102:17; Isaiah 5:7; James 5:4).

Earlier God has told Abraham that "the sin of the Amorites has not yet reached its full measure" (15:16), so he isn't ready to punish the Amorites at this time. But now, the sins of Sodom have indeed reached the point where a righteous God must punish them. Throughout the ages God has shown mercy to peoples that have sinned (Exodus 34:6-7; Lamentations 3:22; Jonah 4:2; Romans 2:4; 3:25; 9:22; 1 Timothy 1:16). If God destroyed us for our sins, who would remain? (Psalm 130:3-4). But God is merciful, giving us a chance to repent. Nevertheless, Sodom's days are numbered. There is a time that judgment must fall and that time has come.

Abraham is under no illusions. He *knows* how bad Sodom really is (13:13). He *knows* how truly wicked the city and its leaders are, evidenced by the fact that he refused to accept anything from the king of Sodom (14:21-24). He *knows* that when the Lord's angels observe the sins of the city, he will be obligated by all that is right and holy to destroy it. But Abraham feels an obligation to protect his own family from that destruction.

Will Not the Judge of All the Earth Do Right? (Exodus 18:22-25)

Now we see a most amazing, bold, audacious appeal from Abraham to Yahweh. "The men turned away and went toward Sodom, but Abraham remained standing before the LORD. Then Abraham approached him and said:

---

[1] Leon J. Wood, *zā'aq*, TWOT #570a. The roots *zā'aq* and *sā'aq* are very similar, both signifying the same sense of a cry for help out of a situation of distress.

"Will you sweep away the righteous with the wicked? What if there are fifty righteous people in the city? Will you really sweep it away and not spare the place for the sake of the fifty righteous people in it? Far be it from you to do such a thing – to kill the righteous with the wicked, treating the righteous and the wicked alike. Far be it from you! Will not the Judge of all the earth do right?" (Exodus 18:22-25)

Abraham's name for God – "The Judge of All the Earth" – is another indication of Abraham's monotheism and very high view of God's righteousness. The gods in the Mesopotamian pantheon were not known for their righteousness, but for their capriciousness and sins. On the contrary, Yahweh is the righteous and holy God! He can be trusted to do what is right. Abraham is sure of it.

God has just spoken about Abraham's destiny to raise up his family in "doing what is right and just (*mishpāt*)" (18:19). Now Abraham demands righteousness of God: "Will not the Judge (*shāpat*) of all the Earth do right (*mishpāt*)?" (18:25). The term "judge" is *shāpat*, "judge, govern, act as ruler," is from the same word group as *mishpāt*, "judgment, justice" in verse 18.[2] How can God destroy a city that has 50 righteous residents? He asks. It would be wrong "to kill the righteous with the wicked," Abraham contends. If God expects justice of Abraham, surely he himself must be just, Abraham argues. Abraham maintains from God's own character that God must treat the righteous justly.

Q1. What is the basis of Abraham's argument that God should spare Sodom? How does it relate to God's character?

http://www.joyfulheart.com/forums/index.php?act=ST&f=85&t=350

Abraham's motive in this appeal, of course, is to save his nephew Lot from destruction along with Sodom. This is the second time Abraham has risked himself to rescue Lot. Now he comes before the Lord himself with incredible nerve and chutzpah!

Was God upset with Abraham's boldness? No. I think God had set up Abraham for this very act of intercession by revealing to Abraham his intentions for Sodom.

Boldness Mixed with Humility

Over the course of the next few minutes, Abraham boldly bargains God down from 50 to 10 righteous people that would prevent God from destroying Sodom – and the Lord agrees. Abraham dares go no lower.

[2] Robert D. Culver, *mishpāt*, TWOT #2443 and #2443c.

Throughout this bold prayer, Abraham asks for the Lord's indulgence, repeatedly acknowledging his own humble place before Almighty God:

"Now that I have been so bold as to speak to the LORD, though I am nothing but dust and ashes...." (18:27)

"May the LORD not be angry, but let me speak...." (18:30)

"Now that I have been so bold as to speak to the LORD...." (18:31)

"May the LORD not be angry, but let me speak just once more...." (18:32)

Here is a fine balance of humility, knowing our place, and yet boldness, taking the opportunity that God has given by inviting us to intimacy with him, the King of Heaven. This is praying with two factors in mind: (1) the joy of having God as our Father and (2) maintaining the realization of God's awesomeness ("who art in heaven") and holiness ("hallowed by thy name").

Q2. How did Abraham demonstrate his humility before God? Why must boldness be tempered with humility?

http://www.joyfulheart.com/forums/index.php?act=ST&f=85&t=351

Why Does God Bargain with Abraham?

Why does God bargain with Abraham? God could have said, "What I plan is just – because I say so!" Certainly, God *is* the Judge of All the Earth. He would have been justified in destroying that wicked city and all who chose to live in it. Or he could have said, "Abraham, frankly there aren't even ten just people in Sodom. Don't waste your breath." Be he didn't.

Instead he engages in dialog with Abraham to see how far Abraham's faith will take him.

Was the Lord angry with Abraham? Oh, no. Not at all. Abraham is the apple of his eye. He is delighted that his servant Abraham believes in him enough and understands him enough to ask this. Genesis 15:6 explains, "Abraham believed God, and it was reckoned unto him as righteousness." The faith of this pre-Christian human is wonderful to God. Here is a man who actually trusts him enough to pray this kind of prayer. Wow!

God loves you when you pray to him. When you call out, "Abba, Father," he hears your prayers and longs to answer them. After all, you are his child. He has chosen to adopt you into his family and bless you – because of Jesus.

Notice, however, about this bargaining session, that Abraham is not offering to do something in return for God's favor – trying to buy God's response. Instead he is appealing again and again to God's own gracious and righteous character. This is the kind of bargaining that doesn't demean God by cheapening his response into a transaction, but exalts God by magnifying his righteousness, by insisting that his great righteousness requires him to spare the city for even ten righteous persons.

Q3. Do you think Abraham's boldness pleased God? Why or why not? What might cause God to take delight in your prayers to him?

http://www.joyfulheart.com/forums/index.php?act=ST&f=85&t=352

Persistence in Prayer

Abraham's persistence pleases God also. Jesus gave us two parables that teach persistence in prayer – the parable of the Friend at Midnight (Luke 11:5-13) and the Parable of the Persistent Widow (Luke 18:1-8). In both parables, the lesson is the same.

> "I tell you, though he will not get up and give him the bread because he is his friend, yet **because of the man's boldness** he will get up and give him as much as he needs.

> "So I say to you: **Ask** and it will be given to you; **seek** and you will find; **knock** and the door will be opened to you. For everyone who asks receives; he who seeks finds; and to him who knocks, the door will be opened. (Luke 11:8-10)

> "... Yet because this widow **keeps bothering me**, I will see that she gets justice, so that she won't eventually wear me out with her coming!'"

> And the Lord said, "Listen to what the unjust judge says. And will not God bring about justice for his chosen ones, who cry out to him day and night? Will he keep putting them off? I tell you, he will see that they get justice, and quickly. However, when the Son of Man comes, will he find faith on the earth?" (Luke 18:5-8)

An older generation of saints used to call this kind of persistence "praying through," praying until assurance of an answer comes. If we want answers to our prayers, we too must learn to "pray through" and not quit before the assurance of answered prayer comes.

Q4. In what way does Abraham show persistence? Why is persistence necessary in prayer? Have you ever experienced "praying through"? What was it like?

http://www.joyfulheart.com/forums/index.php?act=ST&f=85&t=353

The Audacity of Prayer

Through his prayer, Abraham has prevailed upon the Lord to change his mind – at least to modify his judgment. Last week with Moses we examined the audacious assumption that underlies prayer – that we can influence God to change his mind. Of course, God will never act against his own character and word. But God can work out his will and purpose in many ways.

Notice how God answers. While there are not ten righteous people in Sodom, God answers the *intent* of Abraham's prayer – to save his nephew. Lot is righteous (2 Peter 2:7), so he and the family who comes under Lot's protection must be saved. The angels were under strict orders from God that they were not to destroy Sodom until Lot was safe. When Lot requested permission to only flee as far as Zoar, the angel granted his petition:

> "Very well, I will grant this request too; I will not overthrow the town you speak of. But flee there quickly, because *I cannot do anything* until you reach it." (Genesis 19:21-22)

Abraham prays and God grants the *intent* of his request, even though he does not grant the *literal request* itself. How wonderful! How gracious!

Lessons from Abraham's Intercession

I believe God intended to teach Abraham – and us – several lessons about intercession, that is, praying to God on behalf of someone else. I see four lessons here:

1. **Boldness** or confidence before God is necessary. See Ephesians 2:18; 3:12; Hebrews 4:16; 10:19.
2. **Humility**. Abraham remains respectful of God and cognizant of his own inferiority at the same time that he petitions boldly.
3. **Yahweh's character and word** are the basis of the appeal. You can see this in some of the great prayers of intercession in the Bible: Exodus 32:9-14; 33:12-17; Numbers 16:20-22; 1 Samuel 7:5-14; 2 Samuel 24:17; 1 Kings 17:20-23; 2 Kings 19:1-37; Ezra 9:5-15; Nehemiah 1:4-9; Daniel 9:4-19; Amos 7:2-6.
4. **Persistence** in prayer continues until the answer is received.

I invite you to seek this awesome God in bold, persistent, prevailing prayer, based on his promises and character. Indeed, this is the will of God in Christ Jesus for you! (1 Thessalonians 5:18).

The Intercession of Jesus on Our Behalf

When I think about Abraham interceding for sinful Sodom – especially for his nephew Lot – I think of Christ's constant intercession for us his people before the Father. We read that he is our "Advocate with the Father, Jesus Christ the Righteous" (1 John 2:1). He is the "one Mediator between God and men, the man Christ Jesus" (1 Timothy 2:5). He is "at the right hand of God and is also interceding for us" (Romans 8:34). And he is able to save us to the uttermost "seeing that he ever lives to make intercession for [us]" (Hebrews 7:25).

Perhaps the extent of our sin is not as great as that of Sodom, but certainly our sinfulness before God is just as repugnant. Thank God that there is One who intercedes for us, who has brought us to repentance, and has made a way for us to be forgiven.

Now, like Abraham and Moses and Jesus, we are to intercede for others. We are to stand in the gap for them (Ezekiel 22:30), that they might find salvation. God has called us to intercession. God has called us to prayer.

Prayer

Father, I have been way too timid in my prayers, when I compare myself to Abraham. Help me to know you so well that I won't feel afraid to ask great things of you. Grow my faith in you and lead me to exercise this ever increasing faith in my prayers to you. In Jesus' name, I pray. Amen.

Key Verse

"Then Abraham approached him and said: 'Will you sweep away the righteous with the wicked? What if there are fifty righteous people in the city? Will you really sweep it away and not spare the place for the sake of the fifty righteous people in it? Far be it from you to do such a thing – to kill the righteous with the wicked, treating the righteous and the wicked alike. Far be it from you! Will not the Judge of all the earth do right?'" (Genesis 18:23-25)

4. David's Prayer for Pardon and Confession of Sin (Psalm 51)

From David, a lover of God and at the same time a terrible sinner, comes the most moving prayer for pardon in the Bible. If you've been burdened by sin and guilt, this prayer can serve as a model for you as you put your past behind you and move into a new place in God.

I'm calling this a Prayer for Pardon instead of a Prayer of Confession for a couple of reasons.

Julius Schnoor von Carolsfeld (German artist, 1794-1872), "David's Punishment" by, woodcut illustration in *Das Buch der Bücher in Bilden*.

1. "Prayer of Confession" has a fixed place in our church traditions, thus it is harder to examine.

2. I believe that it is fully possible to pray a prayer of confession without faith. The beauty of David's prayer is that it is above all a bold Prayer for Pardon in which he also confesses his sins.

All in all, it is a beautiful example for us to learn from.

Setting the Scene (2 Samuel 11-12)

The ascription to Psalm 51 reads,

"For the director of music. A psalm of David. When the prophet Nathan came to him after David had committed adultery with Bathsheba."

I take it that this indicates David's authorship of the Psalm. If so, herein lies a story of humble origins, a rise to glory, self-indulgence, moral corruption, and finally David's restoration to the God that he loved.

From boyhood David has loved God. His is a humble life, eighth son in a family of brothers who don't take him seriously. On the hillsides as a shepherd boy he composes songs to the Lord and sings them until the mountain crags echo with praises. But then his life takes a turn. He is called to King Saul's court to sing soothing songs to a troubled monarch. Then he kills the Philistine giant Goliath with a stone from his shepherd's slingshot and vanquishes the Philistine army that had oppressed the land.

Now a military leader, he leads soldiers to fend off Philistine attacks against Israel. The common people sing, "Saul has killed his thousands, but David his ten thousands," and Saul, in jealousy, begins to fear and hate him. David runs for his life, and hides out for years in the rocky fastness of the wilderness and later among his enemies, the Philistines themselves.

Saul is finally killed and David exalted as king. He begins as a righteous ruler, but power and wealth take their toll on his moral compass. One day from the height of his palace, he watches as Bathsheba, wife of Uriah, one of his loyal warriors, bathes on her rooftop. In lust he calls her to the palace and gets her pregnant. When he can't blame her pregnancy on her husband, he has her husband killed. Now outwardly righteous, but inwardly corrupt, he is far from God.

But God is not far from him. One day God sends Nathan the prophet who tells him the simple story of a poor man being cheated by a rich man out of the little ewe lamb that he loves. Enraged, David says, "The man deserves to die."

> Nathan lifts a bony finger, points directly at the corrupt King, says with an even voice, "You are that man," and pronounces the Lord's judgment upon him. This shocks David out his denial and cover-up.

> Then David said to Nathan, "I have sinned (*hātā'*) against the LORD." Nathan replied, "The LORD has taken away your sin (*hattā't*). You are not going to die. But because by doing this you have made the enemies of the LORD show utter contempt, the son born to you will die." (2 Samuel 12:13-14)

The Lord punishes David for his sin, a Father's stern discipline you might call it, but he forgives the sin that had become a wedge between David and his God and restores him to fellowship. The Lord draws him close and David, now chastened, responds.

A Look at Psalm 51

We're going to analyze Psalm 51 together, verse by verse. But to get the big picture, I encourage you to read the Psalm over and over out loud. Pray it to God. Memorize its most memorable lines. Make it your own. Here is my outline of Psalm 51:

1. Pleading for God's mercy (1-2)
2. Confessing and acknowledging sin (3-5)
3. Hungering for a pure heart once more (6-12)
4. Resolving to declare God's grace (13-15)
5. Offering the sacrifice of a contrite heart (16-17)
6. Praying for Jerusalem's prosperity (18-19)

Now let's look at it section by section.

1. Pleading for God's Mercy (Psalm 51:1-2)

"[1]Have mercy on me, O God, according to your unfailing love;
according to your great compassion blot out my transgressions.

[2]Wash away all my iniquity
and cleanse me from my sin." (Psalm 51:1-2)

David begins by calling out for mercy. Why? Because he recognizes that God's revealed character is one of love and compassion. From the time of Moses, God has revealed himself as:

"The Lord, the Lord, the compassionate and gracious God, slow to anger, abounding in love and faithfulness, maintaining love to thousands, and forgiving wickedness, rebellion and sin. Yet he does not leave the guilty unpunished; he punishes the children and their children for the sin of the fathers to the third and fourth generation." (Exodus 34:6-7)

This self-revelation is not just a single occurrence. Throughout the Old Testament and the New, God is known as the God of mercy and compassion. (See, for example, Psalm 86:15; 103:8-10; 145:8; Joel 2:13; Numbers 14:18; Deuteronomy 4:11; Nehemiah 9:17; Micah 7:18.) He is the God who disciplines his children but also forgives and restores them. Some people think the angry God of the Old Testament is vastly different from the loving Father of the New, but they are wrong. God shows his anger against sin in the Old Testament and the New, but is known above all for his mercy.

So David calls upon God's mercy as his sin lies exposed before God.

Mercy and Compassion (51:1)

God owes David no favors; David realizes he is bankrupt. So he begins his prayer:

"Have mercy on me, O God,

according to your unfailing love;

according to your great compassion." (51:1)

"Mercy" (*hānan*) means "be gracious, pity … a heartfelt response by someone who has something to give to one who has a need." Here it is a plea to Yahweh to "be gracious to me."[1] David asks for this mercy in accordance with (that is, on the basis of) God's well-known character qualities of steadfast love and compassion.

"Unfailing love" (NIV), "lovingkindness" (KJV), and "steadfast love" (NRSV) translate the common Hebrew noun *hesed*. In the mid-twentieth century many scholars saw the word as expressing loyalty within a covenant.[2] But the word is more than that. It also carries ideas of love, faithfulness, good-heartedness, kindness. The KJV translation of "lovingkindness" may be a pretty good translation after all.[3]

"Compassion" (NIV), "tender mercies" (KJV), and "mercy" (NRSV) represent the Hebrew noun *rahămîm*, "tender mercy, compassion." The root word "refers to deep love (usually of a 'superior' for an 'inferior') rooted in some 'natural' bond."[4]

A Request for Pardon (51:1b-2)

Now David makes his request:

"Blot out my transgressions.
Wash away all my iniquity
and cleanse me from my sin." (51:1b-2)

This is Spirit-inspired poetry, so in keeping with Hebrew poetic style of synoptic parallelism where two or more lines repeat the same idea, David makes his request with three synonyms for forgiveness and three synonyms for sin.

- Blot out - transgressions

- Wash away - iniquity

- Cleanse - sin

We'll look at some synonyms for sin in a moment. But, first, I am fascinated by the synonyms for pardon.

---

[1] Edwin Yamauchi, *hānan*, TWOT #694.
[2] For example, N.H. Snaith, *The Distinctive Ideas of the Old Testament* (Schocken, 1964), pp. 94-130.
[3] R. Laird Harris, *hesed*, TWOT #698.
[4] Leonard J. Coppes, *rāham*, TWOT #2146a.

"Blot out" (*māhā*) means "wipe, wipe out."[5] The word is used for blotting out the inhabitants of the earth in the flood and erasures in ancient leather scrolls made by washing or expunging. Here and in verse 9 the word seems to suggest "removing a stain."

"Wash away" (NIV, *kābas*) or "wash thoroughly" (KJV, NRSV) means "wash, be washed, perform the work of a fuller," that is "to make stuffs clean and soft by treading, kneading and beating them in cold water."[6] The same verb is found in verse 7b: "Wash me and I will be whiter than snow." The stain of sin is deep and David recognizes his need for radical and deep washing.

"Cleanse" (*tāhēr*) means "be pure, be clean." The word is used of wind sweeping the skies clear and the purifying of silver. It is used of moral purity as well as the ritual purity of the Levites and of holy vessels in the tabernacle.[7] The adjective formed from this verb is used in verse 10 where David asks for a "pure heart" or a "clean heart."

David asks God for a full pardon – and cleansing of his character – based on God's merciful nature. It is a bold and very hopeful prayer prayed by a desperately wounded sinner longing to be restored to fellowship with his God.

Q1. In what way does a prayer for pardon require faith? What is that faith based on? How does a person gain the faith to pray this prayer in confidence?
http://www.joyfulheart.com/forums/index.php?act=ST&f=86&t=354

2. Confessing and Acknowledging Sin (51:3-5)

David does not hide or minimize his sin. He owns up to it fully before God.

"3 For I know my transgressions (*pesha'*),
and my sin (*hattā't*) is always before me.
4 Against you, you only, have I sinned (*hātā'*)
and done what is evil (*ra'*) in your sight,
so that you are proved right when you speak
and justified when you judge.
5 Surely I was sinful ('*āwōn*) at birth,
sinful (*hēt'*) from the time my mother conceived me.

---

5 Walter C. Kaiser, *māhā*, TWOT #1178.
6 KB, p. 422, cited in John N. Oswalt, *kābas*, TWOT #946.
7 Edwin Yamauchi, *tāhēr*, TWOT #792.

> [6] Surely you desire truth in the inner parts;
> you teach me wisdom in the inmost place." (51:3-6)

I won't belabor the words for sin, but David uses a number of synonyms, each with a slightly different flavor and connotation.

Transgression (*pesha'*), "rebellion, revolt," designating those who reject God's authority.[8]

Iniquity (*'āwōn*), "infraction, crooked behavior, perversion, iniquity, etc." from a root that means "to bend, twist, distort."[9]

Sin (*hattā't* and *hēt'*) from the root *hātā'* that means to miss a mark or miss the way.[10]

(Do) evil (*ra'*), "evil, distress, wickedness," the opposite of good.[11]

This isn't time to get into a full discussion of the doctrine of original sin. I don't think David is blaming his sinful human condition, that somehow he just can't help sinning because he is "only human." Rather, he is affirming that he is sinful through and through. He is acknowledging the awfulness of his sin in the clearest possible way by using these various synonyms of sin that describe its convolutions of rebellion, twistedness, missing the way, and wickedness.

As long as we try to excuse ourselves, to rationalize our sins to make them seem somewhat less guilt-worthy, we haven't confessed our sins to God in the way that is necessary. We must own up to our sinful behavior, take full responsibility for it, call it what it actually is, and be sorry for offending God in this way. Then we are ready for grace, but not until.

Notice verse 4:

> "Against you, you only, have I sinned
> and done what is evil in your sight."

Does this mean that David's sin against Bathsheba and her husband Uriah were meaningless, inconsequential? No, not at all. But David recognizes that the greatest sin of all is against the Lord that he purports to love. When he sins, he is flaunting his rebellion in God's face. He is saying to God, who told him that murder and adultery were wrong, that he doesn't care. Yes, we can sin against people and need to make these sins right (Matthew 5:23). But our sin is even more against our heavenly Father. It is that breach that must be healed at all costs.

---

[8] G. Herbert Livingston, *pāsha'*, TWOT #1846a.
[9] Carl Schultz *'āwā*, TWOT #1577a.
[10] G. Herbert Livingston, *hātā'*, TWOT #638e.
[11] G. Herbert Livingston, *rā'a'*, TWOT #2191a.

Q2. In his prayer does David seek to minimize his sins? To maximize them? Why does an authentic prayer for pardon require clear, unvarnished acknowledgement of sin to be effective?
http://www.joyfulheart.com/forums/index.php?act=ST&f=86&t=355

3. Hungering for a Pure Heart Once More (51:6-12)

David has painted his iniquity in clear colors. Now he begins to contrast his own sinfulness with what God desires. He looks within. Sinfulness is not primarily in one's actions, but in one's heart.

"6 Surely you desire truth in the inner parts;
you teach me wisdom in the inmost place.

7 Cleanse me with hyssop, and I will be clean;
wash me, and I will be whiter than snow.

8 Let me hear joy and gladness;
let the bones you have crushed rejoice.

9 Hide your face from my sins and blot out all my iniquity.

10 Create in me a pure heart, O God,
and renew a steadfast spirit within me.

11 Do not cast me from your presence
or take your Holy Spirit from me.

12 Restore to me the joy of your salvation
and grant me a willing spirit, to sustain me." (51:6-12)

Integrity in the Heart (51:6)

In verse 6a David speaks of "the inner parts" (NIV), "the inward parts" (KJV), "the inward being" (NRSV). The Hebrew word *tūhot* describes an object "covered over, hidden, or concealed," carrying the idea of the inner being of a person covered up by the body.[12] The parallel idea in 6b is of an "inmost place" (NIV), "hidden part" (KJV), "secret heart" (NRSV), from the word *sātam*, "stop up, shut up, keep close."[13]

In the New Testament Paul talks about the "inner being" (Romans 7:22), the "new self" (Ephesians 4:24; Colossians 3:9). Peter uses the expression of "the inner self" (NIV, 1 Peter 3:4) or "the hidden man of the heart" (KJV).

---

[12] Ralph H. Alexander, *tûah*, TWOT #795b.
[13] *Sātam*, TWOT #1550.

It is this inner person who must be converted and cleansed and discipled. Our actions (when we are not putting on an act for others) flow from this inner person, from our heart of hearts. Jesus taught:

"For out of the overflow of the heart the mouth speaks. (Matthew 12:34)

"For out of the heart come evil thoughts, murder, adultery, sexual immorality, theft, false testimony, slander." (Matthew 15:19)

So David calls out for "truth in the inner parts" and "wisdom in the inmost place" (51:6).

A Prayer for Deep Cleansing (51:7)

Now he offers a prayer for deep cleansing:

"Cleanse me with hyssop, and I will be clean;
wash me, and I will be whiter than snow." (51:7)

"Cleanse me" translates a word that denotes a cleansing or purifying ceremony during which sin is done away with.[14] Hyssop is a small plant that grows on walls, probably marjoram in the mint family. It was used in purification ceremonies to apply blood and water.[15] David is calling upon God himself, not just a priest, to cleanse him through and through to remove his deeply ingrained sin. If God cleanses him, if God washes him, then he will be "whiter than snow."

A Prayer for the Joy of Salvation (51:8, 12)

"Let me hear joy and gladness;
let the bones you have crushed rejoice." (51:8)

"Restore to me the joy of your salvation." (51:12a)

Being separated from God by sin brings pain in one's spirit, a sense of guilt and estrangement. Contrary to those who cynically perceive Christianity as a guilt-driven religion, God doesn't desire us to live with guilt, but to enjoy forgiveness and full fellowship with him. Here David prays for joy to replace his misery and "the bones you have crushed."

---

[14] The verb *hātā'*, which means "sin, miss the way" in the Qal stem, means in the Piel and Hithpael stems "to make a sin offering" or a cleansing or purifying ceremony during which sin is done away with. G. Herbert Livingston, *hātā'*, TWOT #638.

[15] See Exodus 12:22; Leviticus 14:4-6, 49-52; Numbers 19:6, 17-19; Hebrews 9:19; John 19:29. Herbert Wolf, *'ēzōb*, TWOT #55.

In verse 12a, the word "restore" (*shûb*), "turn back, return," carries the idea of "give back, restore."[16] David has known the joy of God's salvation and rescue before. Now he longs for this joy in fellowship to be restored to him once more. It is his earnest prayer.

Have you lost the "joy" of your salvation? Have you become somewhat distant from God? Have you taken God for granted? Or perhaps have you never really got to know him? God wants to restore the joy to you that is your birthright as a Christian. Joy is a fruit of the Holy Spirit's work in your life (Galatians 5:22-23). Call out to him in repentance and receive the joy God desires for you.

A Prayer for a Pure Heart (51:10, 12b)

Now David prays for a pure heart and a willing spirit.

"Create in me a pure heart, O God,
and renew a steadfast spirit within me." (51:10)

"and grant me a willing spirit, to sustain me." (51:12b)

David uses two interesting words in his prayer in verse 10 – "create" and "pure." "Create" (*bārā'*) in this verse carries the connotation of "to initiate something new."[17]

"Pure" (NIV, *tāhōr*) or "clean" (KJV) comes from a verb we saw in verse 2, "to cleanse," which is used of ritual or moral purity and of the pureness of the unalloyed gold of the temple furniture. The temple chambers which have been defiled (Nehemiah 13:9) are purified.[18] Now the word describes the heart David longs for.

But isn't he asking for too much? David has been a slave to lust, drunk with power, stained by murder. How can he now pray for a pure heart? Isn't it too late? No. Can we be pure again once we've been corrupted? Yes.

Jesus taught us, "Blessed are the pure in heart, for they will see God" (Matthew 5:8). Peter observed, "He made no distinction between us and them, for he purified their hearts by faith" (Acts 15:9). God spoke to Peter, "Do not call anything impure that God has made clean" (Acts 10:15). God is in the heart purification business. The author of Hebrews wrote:

"How much more, then, will the blood of Christ, who through the eternal Spirit offered himself unblemished to God, cleanse our consciences from acts that lead to death, so that we may serve the living God!" (Hebrews 9:14)

---

[16] *Shûb*, BDB 999, Hiphil 1d.

[17] Thomas E. McComiskey, *bārā'*, TWOT #278. A different synonym for "create," is *yāsar*, which suggests "to fashion, to shape something new."

[18] Edwin Yamauchi, *tāhēr*, TWOT #792d.

Do you feel unforgiven? Unforgivable? Jesus died for your sins and he desires to forgive you, no matter what you have done. Pray this prayer with David:

> "Create in me a pure heart, O God,
> and renew a steadfast spirit within me." (51:10)

The second part of verse 10 is a prayer for God to renew (*hādash*, "repair, renew, rebuild"[19]) a "right" (KJV, NRSV, *kûn*) or "steadfast" (NIV) spirit, "established, prepared, made ready, fixed, certain, right."[20]

In verse 12b he prays for a "willing spirit" (NIV, NRSV) or to be upheld by God's "free spirit" (KJV). The adjective *nādīb*, "noble, willing, inclined," is from the root *nādab*, "make willing, incite, an uncompelled and free movement of the will unto divine service or sacrifice."[21] Oh, for a spirit that longs to serve God, a heart that is inclined to him!

Q3. Is it possible to have a pure heart? How does God bring about a pure heart? What is our part in this?
http://www.joyfulheart.com/forums/index.php?act=ST&f=86&t=356

Do Not Take Your Holy Spirit from Me (51:11)

Now David prays against his great fear:

> "Do not cast me from your presence
> or take your Holy Spirit from me." (51:11)

Is it a realistic fear? Is God like that? When David was just a boy, King Saul had sinned and rebelled against God. Shortly after this, the Prophet Samuel had come to his father's farm, directing that all Jesse's sons appear before him:

> "So Samuel took the horn of oil and anointed him in the presence of his brothers, and from that day on the Spirit of the LORD came upon David in power.... Now the Spirit of the LORD had departed from Saul...." (1 Samuel 16:13-14)

The Spirit of God had left Saul and come upon David. So David is terrified that in his sin this would happen to him as well, that God's Spirit will desert him. But he repents and trusts God for the answer to his prayer.

---

[19] Carl Philip Weber, *hādash*, TWOT #613.
[20] John N. Oswalt, *kûh*, TWOT #964. "The root meaning is to bring something into being with the consequence that its existence is a certainty."
[21] Leonard J. Coppes, *nādab*, TWOT #1299b.

4. Resolving to Declare God's Grace (51:13-15)

Now David looks forward to the answer to his prayer and how he will serve God.

" [13] Then I will teach transgressors your ways,
and sinners will turn back to you.
[14] Save me from bloodguilt,[22] O God, the God who saves me,
and my tongue will sing of your righteousness.
[15] O Lord, open my lips,
and my mouth will declare your praise." (51:13-15)

Restored and forgiven, he sees himself once again serving the Lord – teaching, singing, praising. Note that he is not bargaining with God, but anticipating and promising to God what he will do. I don't see this so much as a vow but a vision of the future.

5. Offering the Sacrifice of a Contrite Heart (51:16-17)

Now David compares true repentance to ritual sacrifice.

"You do not delight in sacrifice, or I would bring it;
you do not take pleasure in burnt offerings.
The sacrifices of God are a broken spirit;
a broken and contrite heart,
O God, you will not despise." (51:16-17)

Not Outward Religion (51:16)

Though Israel had a well-developed sacrificial system designed to atone for sin, too often people just went through the motions of religion without real repentance, without a genuine desire for change, without a real love for God. Samuel had told King Saul:

"Does the LORD delight in burnt offerings and sacrifices
as much as in obeying the voice of the LORD?
To obey is better than sacrifice,
and to heed is better than the fat of rams." (1 Samuel 15:22)

You find this theme among several of the later prophets, as well.

"'The multitude of your sacrifices – what are they to me?' says the LORD.
'I have more than enough of burnt offerings,
of rams and the fat of fattened animals;

---

[22] Bloodguilt (*dām*, "blood") was the sin of shedding innocent blood, considered a mortal sin. In David's case, he had ordered the death of Uriah, Bathsheba's husband (TWOT #436; BDB 197, g).

I have no pleasure
in the blood of bulls and lambs and goats.'" (Isaiah 1:11)

"For I desire mercy, not sacrifice,
and acknowledgment of God rather than burnt offerings." (Hosea 6:6)

"With what shall I come before the LORD
and bow down before the exalted God?
Shall I come before him with burnt offerings,
with calves a year old?
Will the LORD be pleased with thousands of rams,
with ten thousand rivers of oil?
Shall I offer my firstborn for my transgression,
the fruit of my body for the sin of my soul?
He has showed you, O man, what is good.
And what does the LORD require of you?
To act justly and to love mercy
and to walk humbly with your God." (Micah 6:6-9)

We Christians also have developed rituals through which we can be absolved from sin. It may be formal confession and absolution by a priest or pastor, or by praying a particular prayer. Confession is important in this process (James 5:16). But whatever shape it takes, God is not looking for outward religious action but for heart repentance and change. In Psalm 51, David fully realizes and celebrates this fact.

But a Broken and Contrite Heart (51:17)

"The sacrifices of God are a broken spirit;
a broken and contrite heart,
O God, you will not despise." (51:17)

"The sacrifices of God" (NIV, KJV) or "The sacrifice acceptable to God" (NRSV) could also be translated, "My sacrifice, O God" (NIV, NRSV footnote).

"Broken" (*shābar*) is used figuratively here of a broken heart.

"Contrite" is *dākă*, a by-form of the verb *dk'*, which also means "to crush," and of *dûk*, "to pound, beat." The verb is consistently used of one who is physically and emotionally crushed because of sin or the onslaught of an enemy.[23] Together, the broken and contrite heart of verse 17 "describe the condition of profound contrition and awe experienced by a sinful person who becomes aware of the divine presence."[24]

---

[23] Herbert Wolf, *dākă*, TWOT #428.
[24] Marvin E. Tate, *Psalms 51-100* (Word Biblical Commentary, Vol. 20; Word, 1990), pp. 28.

Until our hearts break with sorrow at our sin, we are not quite ready for forgiveness. So often we are sad at being caught or exposed, but not sad at hurting the God who loves us or injuring his reputation by our sins. Nathan had told David that his sin had "made the enemies of the LORD show utter contempt" (2 Samuel 12:14). Many conversions these days seem to lack the deep repentance that rends the heart (Joel 2:13). It is not religion, but a relationship that has been injured and must be restored. "Against you, you only, have I sinned and done what is evil in your sight, " David cries (51:4). Oh, that our sins would break our hearts!

Q4. What does it mean to have a broken heart and spirit? Why is this essential in the prayer for pardon? In what sense is this a "sacrifice"? Why do we tend to resist a "broken and contrite heart" in ourselves?
http://www.joyfulheart.com/forums/index.php?act=ST&f=86&t=357

6. Praying for Jerusalem's Prosperity (51:18-19)

The psalm concludes with a prayer for Jerusalem.

"In your good pleasure make Zion prosper;
build up the walls of Jerusalem.
Then there will be righteous sacrifices, whole burnt offerings to delight you;
then bulls will be offered on your altar." (51:18-19)

Assuming that the earlier part of the Psalm was penned by David, these last two verses could have been added after the fall of Jerusalem, as a prayer for the restoration of the city that had been destroyed because of the sin of the nation, recognizing the value of the Psalm as a corporate confession as well as a personal prayer for mercy.[25]

Lessons from a Prayer for Pardon

What do we learn from this Psalm about the prayer to God for pardon?

1. **A prayer for mercy.** He doesn't owe us forgiveness. He offers forgiveness by grace, based on the death of Christ for our sins. We can't bargain for it or promise great deeds in exchange. It is so utterly expensive that it cannot be bought by our

---

[25] So Derek Kidner, *Psalms 1-72* (Tyndale Old Testament Commentaries; InterVarsity Press, 1973), p. 194; and Tate, *Psalms 51-100*, pp. 29-30. Franz Delitzsch (Keil and Delitzsch 5:141-143) defends Davidic authorship of these verses.

promises of future good deeds. It is mercy, pure and simple. A prayer for pardon is a prayer for mercy.

2. **A prayer of boldness**. David's example is a bold prayer asking for full pardon for our sins. We don't minimize or excuse our sins, but confess them honestly and fully before God with no mitigating circumstances. "Let us therefore come boldly unto the throne of grace, that we may obtain mercy, and find grace to help in time of need" (Hebrews 4:16)

3. **A prayer from a broken and contrite heart.** Repentance – confessing our sin, being sorry for it, and turning from it – is necessary to pray the prayer for pardon.

4. **A prayer for inner purity**. In addition to pardon, we are asking for a cleansing of our flawed character so that our hearts might be pure before God. An outward cleansing isn't enough, for God sees the heart and the heart must be changed.

5. **A prayer for the joy of salvation.** When God lifts our sins from us, joy is the result. Our prayer for pardon seeks the joy of unobstructed fellowship and restored access to the presence of God.

6. **A prayer to tell others.** Our prayer for pardon results in a desire to tell others of God's great mercy, a desire to witness to others of God's forgiveness.

Ultimately, the prayer for pardon is a prayer of faith that our Father will restore us. I've often wondered if Judas could have been forgiven. This side of heaven we don't know the answer. But to the best of our knowledge his faith didn't reach out for forgiveness, but languished in the belief that God could not forgive him.

Dear friends, there are many people today who believe God will not forgive them for what they have done. Perhaps you feel this way. David's prayer for pardon is a mighty testimony of the mercy of God and our ability to come to him in prayer when we have sinned. This is very good news to the hopeless and the lost. Share the good news of the prayer for pardon and the God who made a way to forgive.

"Then I will teach transgressors your ways,
and sinners will turn back to you....
O Lord, open my lips,
and my mouth will declare your praise." (51:13, 15)

Prayer

Father, so often we sin and need to run back to you and say we are sorry. Teach us to keep short accounts with you. To quickly come and pray the prayer for pardon to you that we might be restored to you. Thank you for the love and sacrifice of Jesus that made all this possible. In His holy name, we pray. Amen.

Key Verses

"Create in me a pure heart, O God,
and renew a steadfast spirit within me.
Do not cast me from your presence
or take your Holy Spirit from me.
Restore to me the joy of your salvation
and grant me a willing spirit, to sustain me." (Psalm 51:10-12)

"The sacrifices of God are a broken spirit;
a broken and contrite heart,
O God, you will not despise." (Psalm 51:17)

5. David's Prayer of Praise at the End of Life (1 Chronicles 29:9-20)

Prayer isn't just asking God for favors or forgiveness. It is much more than that. A great part of Spirit-inspired prayer is praise, if the Book of Psalms is any indication. On the Day of Pentecost when the Holy Spirit fell upon the church in Jerusalem, people heard them in dozens of languages "declaring the wonders of God in our own tongues" (Acts 2:11). "Wonders" (NIV), "wonderful works" (KJV), and "deeds of power" (NRSV) translate the noun *megaleios*, "greatness, sublimity ... mighty deeds."[1] That is indeed the content of many of the Psalms and the psalm we will examine today – extolling and worshipping God in his greatness, glory, and splendor.

Jan de Bray (Dutch painter, 1627-1697), detail of "David Playing the Harp" (1670), oil on canvas, 142 x 154 cm, private collection.

You probably participate in this kind of worship in some of the great hymns of the faith, such as "Great is thy faithfulness, O God, our Father...." or "O worship the King, all glorious above...." or "Holy, holy, holy, Lord God Almighty, all thy works shall praise thy name in earth and sky and sea...." Some of our modern praise choruses lead us in praise, also. But do you, dear friend, practice this kind of praise in your own personal devotions? You can. I hope from examining this psalm you can learn the elements, and then try them out in your prayers.

---

[1] *Megaleios*, BDAG 622.

Setting the Scene (1 Chronicles 28-29)

Leading up to our passage, the aged and ailing King David calls to his palace all his officials, military leaders, and administrators. Now the weak king stands to his feet to address them concerning the temple to be built during his son Solomon's reign. Then he presents to Solomon from his own personal fortune gold, silver, and bronze in great quantities to build the temple and calls on the leaders and officials present to contribute also. They respond with great generosity.

Giving toward the Future Temple (29:9)

Here's where we pick up the story:

> "The people rejoiced at the willing response of their leaders, for they had given freely and wholeheartedly to the Lord. David the king also rejoiced greatly." (29:9)

The common people are moved to praise when they witness this generous dedication of wealth for the future temple. This verse carries two significant words that relate to praise:

"Rejoice" (*sāmah*) denotes "being glad or joyful with the whole disposition."[2] This is an instinctive response to generous and godly behavior. Our generosity can touch others; so can our stinginess.

"Willing" and **"freely"** (NIV) in verse 9 both translate the verb *nādab*, which "connotes an uncompelled and free movement of the will unto divine service or sacrifice."[3] This word appears again and again in our passage. It reflects God's desire for our worship in giving as well as our worship in praise – uncompelled and free giving of ourselves. Sometimes we give because of a sense of duty. Duty is good; I don't want to discourage duty. But giving out of love, "freely, willingly" is even better. The New Testament equivalent of this is:

> "Each man should give what he has decided in his heart to give, not reluctantly or under compulsion, for God loves a cheerful giver" (2 Corinthians 9:7).

Notice here that leaders – beginning with David himself – set the example of giving. That inspires followers to the same selfless attitude. We leaders need to rededicate ourselves and our finances to God so that we can be leaders in giving, not just in administrative or so-called spiritual things. Giving is as spiritual as it gets, since giving gets to the roots of our faith, our future, and our surrender to God.

---

[2] Bruce K. Waltke, *sāmah*, TWOT #2268.
[3] Leonard J. Coppes, *nādab*, TWOT #1299.

Praise to Yahweh (29:10)

The people have participated in the worship of giving. Now David leads them in praise:

> "David praised the LORD in the presence of the whole assembly, saying,
> 'Praise be to you, O LORD,
> God of our father Israel,
> from everlasting to everlasting.'" (29:10)

There are three important verbs we'll see in this passage that are part of David's vocabulary of praise. Each of them has a different flavor

1. *bārak*, "to bless" (vss. 10, 20)
2. *yādā*, "give thanks" (vs. 13)
3. *hālal*, "praise, boast" (vs. 13, cf. "hallelujah")

We'll examine these and others as we get to them in our text. But let's look at the first. "Praised" (NIV) and "blessed" (KJV, NRSV) is *bārak*, "to bless, to endue with power for success, prosperity, fecundity, longevity, etc."[4] The word is often used in the Bible in connection with the hands, though this passage doesn't mention it. Abraham, Jacob, and Jesus lay on hands to bless children. Both Aaron (Leviticus 9:22) and Jesus (Luke 24:50) lift up their hands in blessing and benediction (from a Latin word, *benedictus*, which means "blessing."). It is not surprising to learn that praying with lifted hands was the common position of prayer for the Israelites, because they were blessing God himself with their hands, hearts, and voices.

Q1. In what way do our prayers of praise "bless" God? What do we mere humans have that God desires in a blessing? What are prayers like, that *don't* include blessing God?

http://www.joyfulheart.com/forums/index.php?act=ST&f=87&t=358

David praised publicly, teaching others how to praise. Now the "sweet psalmist of Israel" (2 Samuel 23:1) begins his psalm. Notice how he begins by speaking of God's qualities, kind of like the way the Lord's Prayer begins by describing God, in this case, his eternal nature:

---

[4] John N. Oswalt, *bārak*, TWOT #285. The verb *bārak* is possibly be related to the verb "to kneel," as the related *berek* means "knee."

"Praise be to you, O LORD, God of our father Israel, [5]
from everlasting[6] to everlasting." (29:10)

Power and Glory (29:11a)

Now he begins to ascribe or attribute to God various qualities of might, strength, and glory.

"Yours, O LORD, is the greatness and the power
and the glory and the majesty and the splendor,
for everything in heaven and earth is yours." (29:11a)

Let's look at some of these qualities:

"Greatness" ($g^e d\hat{u}ll\hat{a}$) is from a root that expresses physical growth as well as increase.[7]

"Power" ($g^e b\hat{u}r\hat{a}$), "might," from a root "commonly associated with warfare and has to do with the strength and vitality of the successful warrior." Here God is seen as the mighty warrior *par excellence*, within a culture that often needed to defend itself with armed combat and valued skilled warriors.[8]

"Glory" (*tip'ārā*), "beauty, glory," comes from a root which means "to beautify, to glorify, to boast."[9]

"Majesty" (*nēsah*, NIV) "victory" (KJV, NRSV), "strength, victory, perpetuity," from a root that denotes "brilliance" and "endurance."[10]

"Splendor" (NIV) and "majesty" (KJV, NRSV) (*hôd*) is a uniquely Hebrew word denoting "awe-inspiring splendor ... splendor, majesty, vigor, glory, honor."[11]

Is praise just flattering God? Buttering him up so you can ask a favor? By no means! Praise is expressing out loud the respect and honor we have for our God. That we are willing to openly declare God's greatness encourages others to see God in this light and honor him as well.

---

[5] Israel here refers to the patriarch Jacob.

[6] "Everlasting" is *'ôlām*, which usually indicates "indefinite continuance into the very distant future, forever, ever, everlasting, evermore, perpetual." Allan A. MacRae, *'ôlām*, TWOT #1631a.

[7] Elmer B. Smick, *gādal*, TWOT #315e.

[8] John N. Oswalt, *gābar*, TWOT #310c.

[9] Victor P. Hamilton, *pā'ar*, TWOT #1726b.

[10] Milton C. Fisher, *nāsah*, TWOT #1402a.

[11] Victor P. Hamilton, *hwd*, TWOT #482a.

Praise also affects us. When we acknowledge God's greatness, it strengthens our own faith. Praise is the language of faith. There is a wonderful verse in which relates praise and God's presence – Psalm 23:3

"But thou *art* holy, *O thou* that inhabitest the praises of Israel." (KJV)

"Yet you are holy, enthroned on the praises of Israel." (NRSV)

"Yet you are enthroned as the Holy One; you are the praise of Israel." (NIV)

"Inhabitest" (KJV) or "enthroned" (NRSV, NIV) is *yāshab*, "sit, remain, dwell."[12] There is a sense in which God's presence is often intensely apparent within the context of a praising congregation. Our praises "enthrone" him here on earth. A sense of awe and love is felt by many in the room. I don't think this is just group think or emotionalism, but a real spiritual manifestation of God's own special presence.

Thine Is the Kingdom and the Power (29:11b)

"Yours, O LORD, is the kingdom;
you are exalted as head over all." (29:11b)

It is significant that David the King acknowledges that the kingdom belongs to God. Many monarchs – and people like you and me – perceive themselves as absolute rulers of their domain. But not David. For him, Yahweh is both the ultimate King and Head.

"Kingdom" (*mamlākā*), from the root for "to rule as king," refers to those who are subject to his rule, his subjects, as well as the right to rule.[13] Israel's understanding of their line of kings was that Yahweh was the true king. The tabernacle in the desert (and later the temple in Jerusalem) depicts the tent of a great desert monarch. The ark is his throne, the Holy of Holies his throne room. The Holy Place typifies where the king would be served with food, incense, and light. Eventually, Israel called for a king (1 Samuel 8:4-9), but it was understood that human kings rule on his behalf, not as substitutes for his rule.

The doxology of the Lord's Prayer (probably inserted by the early church in their use of the Lord's Prayer in a liturgical setting) seems draws its wording from verse 11 of this psalm. See the parallels:

"Yours, O LORD, is the greatness
and the power and the glory
and the power and the glory

---

[12] Walter C. Kaiser, *yāshab*, TWOT #922.
[13] Robert D. Culver, *mālak*, TWOT #1199f.

and the majesty and the splendor,
for everything in heaven and earth is yours." 1 Chronicles 29:11 (NIV)

Yours, O LORD, is the kingdom;
for yours is the kingdom
you are exalted as head over all.
forever. Amen. (Matthew 6:13b, NIV margin)

Head over All (29:11b)

Hebrew poetry, of which this short psalm is an example, doesn't rhyme. Instead it uses parallelism and the rhythm of the language in the poetry. These two lines are an example of synoptic parallelism, where both lines say the essentially the same thing in a slightly different way:

"Yours, O LORD, is the kingdom;
you are exalted as head over all." (29:11b)

The first line acknowledges Yahweh as king, the second exalts him as "head" over all. "Head" (rō'sh), is used here to refer to the "chief" of a family.[14] In the New Testament Christ is referred to as "head of the church" (Ephesians 5:23 and elsewhere).

Exalted One (29:11b)

David speaks of God as "exalted" (nāsā'), from a root which means "lift up, bear, carry, support."[15] God is seen as "lifted up, exalted." Exalt is an important part of our vocabulary of praise. The English word "exalt/exalts/exalted" is used 91 times in the NIV, most often for God or for those whom God exalts. Here are a few examples:

The Song of Moses and Miriam:

"I will sing to the Lord,
for he is highly **exalted**...
He is my God, and I will praise him,
my father's God, and I will **exalt** him." (Exodus 15:1-2, 21)

"Blessed be your glorious name,
and may it be **exalted** above all blessing and praise." (Nehemiah 9:5)

and many times in the Psalms:

"The Lord lives! Praise be to my Rock!
Exalted be God my Savior!" (Psalm 18:46)

---

[14] William White, rō'sh, TWOT #2097.
[15] Walter C. Kaiser, nāsā', TWOT #1421.

> "Be **exalted**, O Lord, in your strength;
> we will sing and praise your might." (Psalm 21:13)

> "Glorify the Lord with me;
> let us **exalt** his name together." (Psalm 34:3)

> "Be **exalted**, O God, above the heavens;
> let your glory be over all the earth." (Psalm 57:5)

> "For you, O Lord, are the Most High over all the earth;
> you are **exalted** far above all gods." (Psalm 97:9)

> "**Exalt** the Lord our God
> and worship at his footstool;
> he is holy." (Psalm 99:5)

> "You are my God, and I will give you thanks;
> you are my God, and I will **exalt** you." (Psalm 118:28)

I could go on, but you get the idea. God exalts man (as in verse 12 below, but God is exalted far above any ruler or celebrity, general, scientist, or author. He is the Exalted One! Part of praise is learning to lift him up – exalt him – with our words and with our heart. The praise chorus by Pete Sanchez Jr. taken from Psalm 97:9 says it all:

> "For Thou, O Lord, art high above all the earth, Thou art exalted far above all gods.
> For Thou, O Lord, art high above all the earth, Thou art exalted far above all gods.
> I exalt Thee, I exalt Thee, I exalt Thee, O Lord.
> I exalt Thee, I exalt Thee, I exalt Thee, O Lord."[16]

Q2. In what way does praise exalt God? Why should we exalt God? What does this exaltation do in us? What does it say about us?

http://www.joyfulheart.com/forums/index.php?act=ST&f=87&t=359

Wealth and Honor from Yahweh (29:12)

Now David continues to attribute or ascribe qualities of strength and power to God.

> "Wealth[17] and honor[18] come from you;
> you are the ruler of all things.

---

[16] "I Exalt Thee," words and music ©1977 by Pete Sanchez Jr.

[17] "Wealth" (NIV, *'ōsher*) and "riches" (KJV, NRSV).

[18] "Honor" (*kābōd*) comes from the root "to be heavy, weighty," and figuratively, "a 'weighty' person in society, someone who is honorable, impressive, worthy of respect." When referring to God *kābōd*, "glory of

In your hands are strength[19] and power[20]
to exalt[21] and give strength[22] to all." (1 Chronicles 29:12)

Consider the praise found in Revelation that takes place continually before God's throne:

"Holy, holy, holy
is the Lord God Almighty,
who was, and is, and is to come." (Revelation 4:8)

"You are worthy, our Lord and God,
to receive glory and honor and power, for you created all things,
and by your will they were created
and have their being." (Revelation 4:11)

"To him who sits on the throne and to the Lamb
be praise and honor and glory and power,
for ever and ever!" (Revelation 5:13)

See the similarities with praise in our psalm and in the Book of Psalms? Praise focuses on who God is, not on our experience or feelings. Praise exalts our God.

Q3. Verses 11 and 12 both attribute various characteristics to God, such as glory, honor, and might. How might you begin to mention God's greatness in your own prayers? Where is this kind of praise found by example in the Lord's Prayer? What are your favorite songs that point to God's greatness?
http://www.joyfulheart.com/forums/index.php?act=ST&f=87&t=360

Thanks and Praise (29:13)

The last two lines of this psalm are parallel to each other:

"Now, our God, we give you thanks,
and praise your glorious name." (29:13)

God" far surpasses any earthly honor, since the near-blinding quality of God's glory fills the earth, and can refer to his very presence and character (John N. Oswalt, *kābēd*, TWOT #943e).

[19] "Strength" (NIV) and "power (KJV, NRSV) is *kôah*, "strength, power, ability, might, force, substance, capacity to act, understood both in physical and figurative terms." When applied to God, this term suggests that he is indeed omnipotent (John N. Oswalt, *khh*, TWOT #973a).

[20] "Might" (*gebûrâ*) which we saw in verse 11, pictures God as the ultimate mighty warrior.

[21] "Exalt" (*gādal*) is the verb "promote, exalt, make powerful, make great" (Elmer B. Smick, *gādal*, TWOT #315).

[22] "Give strength" (*hāzaq*) from the basic meaning "be(come) strong" (Carl Philip Weber, *hāzaq*, TWOT #2388).

Here we see two important words in our praise vocabulary:

"Give thanks" (*yādā*), "to thank," comes from a root meaning, "to acknowledge or confess ... God's character... The verb was predominately employed to express one's public proclamation or declaration (confession) of God's attributes and his works. This concept is at the heart of the meaning of praise – a confession or declaration of who God is and what he does."[23]

"Praise" (*hālal*), "praise, boast." The root connotes being sincerely and deeply thankful for and/or satisfied in lauding a superior quality(ies) or great act(s) of the object. The most frequent use relates to praise the God of Israel, with nearly a third of such passages occurring in the Psalms, often imperative summons to praise.[24] The word "hallelujah" comes from this root.

Everything Comes from You (29:14-16)

Now the poetic praise psalm ends, but David's prayer continues:

"But who am I, and who are my people,
that we should be able to give as generously[25] as this?
Everything comes from you,
and we have given you only what comes from your hand.
We are aliens and strangers in your sight,
as were all our forefathers.
Our days on earth are like a shadow,
without hope. O Lord our God,
as for all this abundance that we have provided
for building you a temple for your Holy Name,
it comes from your hand,
and all of it belongs to you." (29:14-16)

David is marveling that he has been able to give such a quantity of gold and silver for the temple. Eighth son of a shepherd, he began with nothing, not even land to call his own. But God has blessed him and he knows it. It comes from God and belongs to God; David is only a temporary steward of God's abundance: "It comes from your hand, and

---

[23] The basic difference between *yādā* and its synonym *hālal*, is that the latter term tends to stress "acclaim of, boasting of, glorying in" and object, while *yādā* emphasizes "recognition" and "declaration" of a fact, whether good or bad. (Ralph H. Alexander, *yādā*, TWOT #847).

[24] Leonard J. Coppes, *hālal*, TWOT #500.

[25] "Give generously" (NIV), "offer willingly," and "make a freewill offering" (NRSV) is *nādab*, which we first saw in verse 9 and occurs twice in verse 17 (Leonard J. Coppes, *nādab*, TWOT #1299).

all of it belongs to you" (29:16). Moses warned the people about overpossessiveness 3,500 years ago as they were about ready to enter the Promised Land:

> "You may say to yourself, 'My power and the strength of my hands have produced this wealth for me.' But remember the Lord your God, for it is he who gives you the ability to produce wealth, and so confirms his covenant, which he swore to your forefathers, as it is today." (Deuteronomy 8:17-18)

While we believe this theoretically, we are very tempted (1) to believe that we earned our own way by the sweat of our own brow and (2) to hold our possessions tightly as our own. This is where we get in trouble with God. It is at this very point that we balk at tithing a full 10%, for example, because we believe that our wealth belongs to us rather than to God. David's prayer reminds us: "It comes from your hand, and all of it belongs to you" (29:16).

The first verse of an old hymn by William W. How says it well:

> "We give Thee but Thine own,
> Whate'er the gift may be;
> All that we have is Thine alone,
> A trust, O Lord, from Thee."[26]

Q4. Why is a person's attitude with regard to giving related to that person's attitude towards praise? Why does an attitude of possessiveness with regards to giving get in the way of worship? In what sense do all your possessions belong to God? What then should be your relationship to your possessions? How will these truths re-energize your giving? Your praise?

http://www.joyfulheart.com/forums/index.php?act=ST&f=87&t=361

Giving Willingly and Honestly (29:17)

David rejoices at how the people have given:

> "I know, my God, that you test the heart
> and are pleased with integrity.[27]
> All these things have I given willingly
> and with honest intent.

---

[26] "We Give Thee but Thine Own," words by William W. How (1864).

[27] "Integrity" (NIV, *yōsher*) and "uprightness" (KJV, NRSV) has the idea of "uprightness, straightness," from a root that denotes going on a straight path (Donald J. Wiseman, *yāshar*, TWOT #930b).

And now I have seen with joy
how willingly your people who are here have given to you." (29:17)

Prayer for Solomon and the People (29:18-19)

Now David prays that this willingness and generosity towards God continue among the people after he is gone. He also prays for his son Solomon, who will ascend to the throne at his father's death.

"O LORD, God of our fathers Abraham, Isaac and Israel,
keep this desire in the hearts of your people forever,
and keep their hearts loyal to you.
And give my son Solomon the wholehearted devotion[28]
to keep your commands, requirements and decrees
and to do everything to build the palatial structure
for which I have provided." (29:18-19)

Praise and Worship (29:20)

Finally, David calls the people to praise the Lord, too.

"Then David said to the whole assembly, 'Praise the LORD your God.' So they all praised the LORD, the God of their fathers; they bowed low and fell prostrate before the LORD and the king." (29:20)

Candidates for Catholic priesthood lie prostrate in the service of ordination.

"Praise" and "bless" in verse 20 is *bārak*, which is used in verse 10 above. But here is our final praise vocabulary word for today. Notice the people's posture – bowing low[29] and falling prostrate. This last word "fell prostrate" (*hāwā*, NIV) or "prostrated

---

[28] "Wholehearted devotion" (NIV, *shālēm*), "perfect heart" (KJV), and "single mind" (NRSV) use the Hebrew word for "heart" along with the verb "be complete, sound," carrying the idea of completion and fulfillment, of entering into a state of wholeness and unity, a restored relationship." The Hebrew noun *shālōm*, "peace, wholeness," comes from this word group (G. Lloyd Carr, *shālēm*, TWOT #2401).

[29] "Bow" (*qādad*), refers to "bowing of one's head accompanying and emphasizing obeisance," emphasizing devotion and deep awe (Leonard J. Coppes, *qādad*, TWOT #1985).

themselves" (NRSV) is usually translated as "worship" in the Old Testament. It is the posture of complete submission before a superior.[30] To bow oneself low before God is the essence of worship. Kneeling and bowing low is the common Muslim prayer posture. But Christians only bow their heads in prayer, except in Catholic and Anglican churches that have kneelers. Why is this? Priests in the Catholic tradition lie completely prostrate at their ordination. Consider trying this posture in your prayers – not as your only posture, but as a sign and symbol of your deep worship and surrender to God.

We have studied David's last recorded prayer, a prayer at the end of life. It is a psalm of praise, a song extolling the attributes of God, a prayer of wonder at God's rich blessings, a prayer for the next king, and a call to deep worship. What can you incorporate in your prayers that you have learned from this prayer?

Prayer

O Lord, sometimes our worship seems so half-hearted, our praise so faint. Teach me, teach us to praise you with all our heart, soul, mind, and strength. Make us a people of praise, who love to praise you. And teach us to hold only loosely the wealth you have entrusted to us. Help us to give willingly and freely, we pray. In Jesus' name. Amen.

Key Verses

"Yours, O Lord, is the greatness and the power
and the glory and the majesty and the splendor,
for everything in heaven and earth is yours.
Yours, O Lord, is the kingdom;
you are exalted as head over all." (1 Chronicles 29:11)

"O Lord our God, as for all this abundance
that we have provided for building you a temple for your Holy Name,
it comes from your hand, and all of it belongs to you." (1 Chronicles 29:16)

---

[30] This Eshtaphal stem of *hāwā* means "to prostrate oneself, to worship." The verb originally meant to prostrate oneself on the ground, a common act of submission before a superior, similar to Muslim prayer with an elaborately prescribed *suğûd* in which the forehead must touch the ground. The Greek equivalent is *proskyneō*, which can mean either "prostration" or "worship" (Edwin Yamauchi, *hāwā*, TWOT #619).

6. David's Psalm of Surrender to the Searcher (Psalm 139)

Many psalms in the Bible mix praise and petition. You'll have a paean of praise, then an earnest petition, a dialog between the psalmist and God. As we get to know God better, our prayers often include discussions with God of the situations in our lives, the things we are struggling with, often concluding with a deliberate request of God for help.

The psalm we'll consider today is one of those dialog psalms – and one of the most moving and beautiful psalms in the whole Bible. The inscription attributes it to David. Let's examine it.

Remember that we are reading inspired Hebrew poetry that relies heavily on parallelism. Don't be intimidated by the beauty and eloquence of it. Look for the thoughts. Look at this as a dialog going on in the

"Der Psalter," woodcut from illustrated German Bible, by R.S., unknown artist.

psalmist's mind. How would you express these thoughts to God in your own way? When you see this as a give and take, a dialog, a discussion or dispute with God that is finally resolved by a prayer of surrender, then it becomes a prayer that you can learn from.

Yahweh the Searcher (139:1-4)

"¹O LORD, you have searched me and you know me.

²You know when I sit and when I rise;

you perceive my thoughts from afar.

[3]You discern my going out and my lying down;
you are familiar with all my ways.

[4]Before a word is on my tongue
you know it completely, O LORD." (139:1-4)

The psalm begins in verse 1 with two verbs, "search" and "know," and ends with the very same verbs in verse 23. The psalm is about God's probing deep into a man's character, sometimes a most unpleasant, uncomfortable exercise (cf. Jeremiah 12:3).

The first word is "searched," Hebrew *hāqar*, which "always connotes a diligent, difficult probing." The word is used for investigating legal cases or the plight of the needy, examining proverbs, looking for information about a city or country, etc. God searches us, probes the heart, examines the mind, and knows us (Jeremiah 17:10; Job 13:9; Psalm 44:21).[1]

The second word is "know/known," the common verb *yāda'*, "know, discern, recognize." Here it is used to express acquaintance with a person.[2]

"[2] You know (*yāda'*) when I sit and when I rise;
you perceive[3] my thoughts from afar.
[3] You discern[4] my going out and my lying down;
you are familiar[5] with all my ways.
[4] Before a word is on my tongue
you know (*yāda'*) it completely, O LORD. (Psalm 139:2-4)

David is acutely aware that God knows his thoughts before he thinks them, his words before he speaks them. God knows his plans, his errands, his comings and goings, his strengths, his weaknesses, even his secret sins – literally everything about him.

---

[1] Herbert Wolf, *hāqar*, TWOT #729b.

[2] Paul R. Gilchrist, *yāda'*, TWOT #848.

[3] *Bîn*, "understand, consider, perceive, prudent, regard" (Louis Goldberg, *bîn*, TWOT #239).

[4] "Discern" (NIV), "search out" (NRSV), and "compassest" (KJV), *zārā*, means literally "scatter, winnow, sift," used here metaphorically perhaps as "examine," in the way that threshed grain is winnowed by tossing it in the wind to separate the wheat from the chaff. "The difficult usage in Psalm 139:3 may be a semantic extension of this root in the sense of "examine" or, as BDB suggest and KB and Dahood (in Anchor Bible, *Psalms III*) affirm, may be a denominative verb *zārā* "to measure" from the noun *zeret* "span" (R. Laird Harris, *zārā*, TWOT #579. Leslie C. Allen, *Psalms 101-150* (Word Biblical Commentary; Word, 1983), p. 250).

[5] *Sākan*, "be of use, service, profit," in verse 3, translated "familiar" (NIV) and "acquainted" (NRSV, KJV). Here it "suggests God's superintending care of the believer" (R.D. Patterson, *sākan*, TWOT #1494).

Hemmed In by God (139:5-7)

David seems a bit of frustrated by this, like you might if you knew your phone was being bugged and you were under constant surveillance.

"You hem me in – behind and before;
you have laid your hand upon me." (139:5)

"Hem in" (NIV, NRSV) and "beset" (KJV) is *sûr*, "bind, besiege," "This root means to make secure a valuable object, such as money."[6] The valued object here is David himself, watched, guarded. If you can imagine what it might be like to be guarded 24 hours a day by teams of Secret Service agents, kept out of harm's way, insulated from danger, perhaps you get a bit of his frustration. He appreciates it, but.... He can't understand such intimate knowledge.

"Such knowledge is too wonderful for me,
too lofty for me to attain." (139:6)

Now he wonders out loud if there is any escape from God.

"Where can I go[7] from your Spirit?
Where can I flee from your presence?" (139:7)

Not that he particularly wants to escape, but he is feeling constricted. You've felt that way, too, when you are tempted with a favorite sin, but know you shouldn't give in because God is watching. It sounds crazy, doesn't it? But sometimes we chafe under God's scrutiny. People have been fleeing from God ever since Adam and Eve and the Garden of Eden (Genesis 3:8) and the prophet Jonah fled from his destiny in Nineveh (Jonah 1:1-3).

"Flee" is *bārah*, "flee, run away." Basically, *bārah* means "to go or pass through" and "to flee or hurry." It occurs mostly in narratives, referring to flight from an enemy.[8] But when God has laid his hand on you, there is no place to run.

Q1. (139:7) Why do people sometimes want to flee from God? Why do people imagine that God doesn't know what they do? Have you ever felt this way?
http://www.joyfulheart.com/forums/index.php?act=ST&f=89&t=366

---

[6] John E. Hartley, *sûr*, TWOT #1898.
[7] "Go" is *hālak*, "go, walk" (*hālak*, TWOT #498).
[8] Earl S. Kalland, *bārah*, TWOT #284.

The Omnipresent God (139:8-10)

Annoyance isn't all the psalmist is feeling. He is overcome with awe at God's omnipresence. "The psalmist, wherever he went, would find himself confronted with a God who was already there," says Allen. "As a man he can be only one place in the world at once, but God is everywhere."[9]

> "8 If I go up to the heavens, you are there;
> if I make my bed in the depths, you are there.
> 9 If I rise on the wings of the dawn, if I settle on the far side of the sea,
> 10 even there your hand will guide me,
> your right hand will hold me fast." (139:8-10)

"The depths" (NIV), "hell" (KJV), or "Sheol" (NRSV) is the Hebrew noun *sh^e'ôl*. There is much dispute about the exact meaning of the word, though it obviously refers to the place of the dead. Both good men and bad men go there (Genesis 37:35; Numbers 16:30). Probably it originally meant "the grave," and only later became a specialized word for "hell."[10]

In the heavens or the in the grave, God is present with us. The sea was often a thing of danger and fear for the Israelites, who were not seagoing people. So to "settle on the far side of the sea," would be to have passed through much danger and be far away from home.

The phrase "rise on the wings of dawn" is an evocative, poetic expression. "Wing" (*kānāp*) is an appendage of a bird with which it flies, "denoting speed as well as protection." David sees the speed with which the sun of dawn travels from East to West.[11] Even though he could quickly travel far, far away, God will be there, too.

Dear friend, are you feeling alone or lonely right now? You may be cut off from human companionship for a time, but God is ever present. There's no place you can go to get rid of him, shake him off your trail, keep him away from your side. He is with you

---

[9] Allen, *Psalms 101-150*, p. 251.

[10] R. Laird Harris, *shā'al*, TWOT #2303c. Allen observes, "The accessibility of Sheol to Yahweh receives a dual treatment in the Old Testament. It is often denied in a stress that fellowship with God and enjoyment of his blessing are confined to this life. While it is not within Yahweh's sphere of blessing, it is within his sphere of sovereignty" (Allen, *Psalms 101-150*, p. 251).

[11] John N. Oswalt, *knp*, TWOT #1003a. Delitzsch understands it this way: "If I should lift wings such as the dawn of the morning has, i.e. could I fly with the swiftness with which the dawn of the morning spreads itself over the eastern sky, towards the extreme west and alight there" (Franz Delitzsch, *Psalms, in loc.*, Keil and Delitzsch, vol. 5, Psalms vol. 3, p. 347). He also notes the expressions wings of the sun (Malachi 4:2) and wings of the wind (Psalm 18:10).

– forever! "I will never leave you or forsake you" (Hebrews 13:5; Deuteronomy 31:6, 8; Psalm 37:25, 28; Isaiah 41:10, 17).

The Strong and Tender Hand of God (139:10-12)

Notice how the psalmist speaks of God's hand. In verse 5 he says:

"You hem me in – behind and before;
you have laid your hand upon me." (139:5)

For God to "lay his hand" on someone could be for harm (Genesis 22:12; 37:22; Exodus 7:4; 24:11; 1 Samuel 23:17; 26:9, 11, 23; Esther 8:7; 9:2; Isaiah 11:14; Ezekiel 39:21, etc.) or for blessing (Genesis 19:16; Ezra 8:31), depending on the context. Here it seems to be positive, since in verse 10 he says:

"... even there your hand will guide me,
your right hand will hold me fast."

God's hand is upon David for good. "Guide" is *nāḥā*, "lead, guide, "the conducting of one along the right path,"[12] also used in verse 24. "Hold" or "hold fast" is *'āḥaz*, "take hold of, seek, grasp."[13] God's grip will not slip, no matter what the danger. God's guidance will be clear, no matter how much fog might obscure the path. Even pitch blackness is of no concern to God (Job 34:22; Hebrews 4:13). I love this passage:

"If I say, 'Surely the darkness will hide me
and the light become night around me,'
even the darkness will not be dark to you;
the night will shine like the day,
for darkness is as light to you." (139:11-12)

Are you undergoing depression, anxiety, persecution, the pain of separation from one you love, failure and defeat, utter desolation? If so, know this: No matter how black it is to you, no matter how impossible it seems, the path is clear to God. This morning in the car I found myself singing that 1976 praise chorus taken from Jeremiah 32:17, KJV):

"Ah, Lord God, thou hast made the heavens
And the earth by thy great power.
Ah Lord God, thou has made the heavens
And the earth by thy outstretched arm.
Nothing is too difficult for thee.
Nothing is too difficult for thee.

---

[12] *Nāḥā*, TWOT #1314.
[13] Herbert Wolf, *'āḥaz*, TWOT #64.

> Great and mighty God,
> Great in power and mighty in strength!
> Nothing, nothing, absolutely nothing,
> Nothing is too difficult for thee!"[14]

No matter where you are or what is going on in your life, God is with you and his might and power are active on your behalf. Hallelujah!

Q2. (139:5, 10). In verses 5 and 10, how does God's hand touch the psalmist? Have you ever felt God's hand on you in a special way? Was it for your good? What was it like?
http://www.joyfulheart.com/forums/index.php?act=ST&f=89&t=367

The Creator of My Inner Person (139:13-16)

The psalmist has considered knowledge of his ways and paths. Now he examines God's intimate knowledge of his very beginnings, his formation, and his inner being.

> "[13] For you created my inmost being;
> you knit me together in my mother's womb.
> [14] I praise you because I am fearfully and wonderfully made;
> your works are wonderful, I know that full well.
> [15] My frame was not hidden from you when I was made in the secret place.
> When I was woven together in the depths of the earth,
> [16] your eyes saw my unformed body.
> All the days ordained for me were written in your book
> before one of them came to be." (139:13-16)

Let's meditate on this beautiful passage for a moment to see God's intricate and tender care for us in the womb.

> "For you created my inmost being;
> you knit me together in my mother's womb." (139:13)

"Created" (NIV), "possessed" (KJV), and "formed" (NRSV) is *qānā*, which here (and 5 other places in the Old Testament) appears to mean "create."[15] God has made the heavens and the earth by his great power, but also the tiniest parts of a tiny human while still an embryo, a fetus. God's awesome power extends to the smallest detail.

---

[14] "Ah, Lord God," words and music by Kay Chance, ©1976 by Kay Chance.
[15] Leonard J. Coppes, *qānā*, TWOT #2039.

"Inmost being" (NIV), "inward parts" (NRSV), and "reins" (KJV) is *kilyâ*, "kidney," then a symbol of the innermost being.[16]

> "... You knit me together in my mother's womb." (139:13b)

The psalmist uses a fascinating word, here translated "knit together" (NIV, NRSV) and "covered" (KJV). The verb is *śākak* (also in Job 10:11), which probably means "weave together," parallel to "woven together" in verse 15, an allusion to cloth woven with different colored threads.[17] Imagine a weaver, an artist in cloth, weaving an intricate pattern, and you see God's love and care.

> "I praise you because I am fearfully and wonderfully made;
> your works are wonderful,
> I know that full well." (139:14)

"Fearfully" is *yārē'*, which means "fear, revere," here in the sense of reverence or awe.[18] "Wonderfully" is *pālā*, "be distinct, marked out,"[19] while "wonderful" (NIV, NRSV) and "marvelous" (KJV) is the verb *pālā'*, "to be wonderful" (spelled slightly differently in Hebrew than *pālā*), from a root that refers to things that are unusual, beyond human capabilities.[20]

The psalmist regards his formation inside his mother with awe and reverence. He is "distinct and marked out," now as he was from the time of his creation. God's work is amazing. When you hold your firstborn in your arms and count all the tiny fingers and toes, you feel what the psalmist was feeling. Awe, amazement, wonder at the miracle of conception, formation, and birth. Wow!

But he continues:

> "My frame was not hidden from you
> when I was made in the secret place.
> When I was woven together in the depths of the earth,
> your eyes saw my unformed body." (139:15-16a)

"The depths of the earth" are "a metaphor here for deepest concealment, i.e., the hiddenness of the womb."[21]

---

[16] John N. Oswalt, *klh*, TWOT #983a.
[17] *Śākak*, TWOT #2260. Allen, *Psalms 101-150*, p. 251.
[18] Andrew Bowling, *yārē'*, TWOT #907.
[19] Victor P. Hamilton, *pālā*, TWOT #1722.
[20] As such, it awakens astonishment (*pl'*) in man. Victor P. Hamilton, *pālā'*, TWOT #1768.
[21] Derek Kidner, *Psalms 73-150* (Tyndale Old Testament Commentaries; InterVarsity Press, 1975), p. 466.

"Woven together" (NIV), "intricately woven" (NRSV), and "curiously wrought" (KJV) is *rāqam*, "variegate, weave with variegated threads, also with threads of gold and silver,"[22] "suggesting the complex patterns and colors of the weaver or embroiderer."[23]

Finally, we see a hint of predestination, or at least God's numbering of the psalmist's days before he is ever born:

> "All the days ordained for me were written in your book
> before one of them came to be." (139:16b)

"Ordained" (NIV), "fashioned" (KJV), and "formed" (NRSV) is *yāsar*, "fashion, form, frame," used in parallel with *bāra'* "create" and *'aśâ* "make" in a number of passages. The word is also used of God's framing or devising something in his mind, of his preordained purposes.[24] Here, determination of length of life is evidently in view.[25]

Q3. (139:13-16) How does an awareness of God's involvement in your prenatal development meant to encourage you? What might this mean to a young woman carrying a child? A young father-to-be? Why is such knowledge overwhelming to us?
http://www.joyfulheart.com/forums/index.php?act=ST&f=89&t=368

God's Precious Thoughts (139:17-18)

Do we resent God's intimate connection to us as an invasion of privacy, an intrusion on our "space"? We could, and sometimes do. But the psalmist rather sees God's personal forming of his body and person as an awesome revelation of the immensity of God's "brain" and attention to the same kind of detail with every human being. Multiply "2000 parts" times 8 billion living human beings and you begin to get the picture that David sees here:

> "How precious to me are your thoughts, O God!
> How vast is the sum of them!
> Were I to count them,
> they would outnumber the grains of sand." (139:17-18a)

---

[22] *Rāqam*, KB 909.
[23] Kidner, *Psalms 73-150*, p. 466.
[24] Thomas E. McComiskey, *yāsar*, TWOT #898.
[25] Allen, *Psalms 101-150*, p. 252.

The intricacy of God's thoughts[26] is "precious" (NIV, KJV) and "weighty" (NRSV), Hebrew *yāqar*, "be precious, valuable, costly, esteem," from a root that conveys the idea of "heavy, honor, dignity."[27]

David finishes this section with a word of reassurance:

> "When I awake,
> I am still with you." (139:18b)

Sleep can sometimes be fearful for children, especially when they have been raised on the prayer, "... and if I die before I wake, I pray the Lord my soul to take." David sleeps and when he awakes, he realizes with joy and comfort, "I am still with you." You and I may wake one morning and find ourselves in heaven, but it will nevertheless be true, "I am still with you." There is a comfort in God's mercy.

Hating God's Enemies (139:19-22)

The next section we find somewhat difficult this side of the cross:

> "[19] If only you would slay the wicked, O God!
> Away from me, you bloodthirsty men!
> [20] They speak of you with evil intent;
> your adversaries misuse your name.
> [21] Do I not hate those who hate you, O LORD,
> and abhor those who rise up against you?
> [22] I have nothing but hatred for them;
> I count them my enemies." (139:19-22)

"Hate" is *śānē'*, "hate, to be hateful.... It expresses an emotional attitude toward persons and things which are opposed, detested, despised and with which one wishes to have no contact or relationship. It is therefore the opposite of love."[28]

Jesus taught us Christians to "love your enemies and pray for those who persecute you, that you may be sons of your Father in heaven..." (Matthew 5:44-45a). But David's sentiment has something to say to us. Sometimes we find ourselves siding with God's enemies, those who go their own way. We must be careful to "hate evil" (Psalm 97:10) as God does, and not be so tolerant that we embrace it and condone it.

---

[26] "Thoughts" is *rēa'*, "purpose, aim," (TWOT #2187), both here and in verse 2.
[27] John E. Hartley, *yāqar*, TWOT #905.
[28] Gerard van Groningen, *śānē'*, TWOT #2272.

Petition: Search Me and Test Me (139:23-24)

Now, after 22 verses of pondering, being annoyed by, and being awed by God's personal focus on his life, David seems to drop to his knees in surrender and pray from the bottom of his heart:

"[23] Search me, O God, and know my heart;
test me and know my anxious thoughts.
[24] See if there is any offensive way in me,
and lead me in the way everlasting." (139:23-24)

Consider this prayer. We saw the key words "search" (*ḥāqar*) and "know" (*yāda'*) in verse 1; now we return to them as the core of our petition. David not only prays that God may search and know him. He prays for God's deep probing and refining. "Test" (NIV, NRSV) or "try" (KJV) is *bāhan*, "examine, try, prove." It often occurs in parallel with "put to the test, tempt" (*nāsā*) or "smelt, refine" (*ṣārap*), and falls in between these two.[29]

Only a person who has come to trust God can sincerely pray for God to refine him or her. Refining is arduous. Refining is painful. But the loving probing and discipline of God eventually yields "the peaceful fruit of righteousness to those who have been trained by it" (Hebrews 12:11).

Do you feel some anxiety praying such a vulnerable prayer? So did David: "Test me and know my anxious thoughts," he prays. "Anxious thoughts" (NIV) or "thoughts" (KJV, NRSV) is *śar'appîm*, "disquieting thoughts."[30] This prayer may be breaking new ground for you. You may have been resistant or at best passive about praying this way. Perhaps you've heard the common Christian admonition, "Don't pray for patience, because God will send you trials" – and who wants trials? But with David, as you've learned to trust the seeking, questing, probing God, you are now able to surrender yourself to him willingly, actively to his refining care.

David prays, "See if there is any offensive way in me" (139:24a). "Offensive" (NIV), "wicked" (KJV, NRSV), and "hurtful" (NRSV margin) are *'ōṣeb*, "sorrow."[31] Often with our acute sense of guilt we are unwilling for God to reveal more sin and impurity; we are overwhelmed with what we see already! But now, as trusting children, we ask our

---

[29] *Bāhan* is used mainly in the spiritual or religious realm with God as the subject and man as the object, denoting attaining knowledge intellectually or intuitively (John N. Oswalt and Bruce K. Waltke, *bāhan*, TWOT #230).

[30] *Ś'p*, TWOT #2273.

[31] "Hurtful way," BDB 780. The root word *'āsab* could be could be either "to worship" or "to cause pain." Ronald B. Allen, *'āsab*, TWOT #1666b or #1667b. Allen translates it, "See if I have been behaving as an idolater."

Father to reveal those things in us which may offend him or be hurtful to us. And in his gentleness, God answers our prayer.

The Path Leading into Eternity (139:24b)

"... And lead me in the way everlasting." (139:24b)

When you come down to it, this fearful prayer for refining is a prayer in our own interest. This is the manner in which God can fit us for a life that stretches on and on into God's forever present – eternity.[32]

The Bible calls it a "way," *derek*, "way, road." Since it comes from a root meaning "to tread, trample," it refers to "a path worn by constant walking." It is often used metaphorically of the actions and behavior of men who follow the way of the righteous or the way of the wicked.[33]

Jesus instructed his disciples:

"Enter through the narrow gate.
For wide is the gate and broad is the road that leads to destruction,
and many enter through it.
But small is the gate and narrow the road that leads to life,
and only a few find it." (Matthew 7:13-14)

You want to be on the right path, not the wrong path. You don't want to be deceived about eternity, do you? And so, you pray that awesome, trusting prayer to Jesus, the Guide: "Lead me in the way everlasting" (139:24b). "Lead" is *nāḥā*, "lead, guide, "the conducting of one along the right path," which we saw in verse 10.[34]

I am distinctly aware as I am writing this that God is speaking directly to individuals. Perhaps you've never prayed this kind of prayer before because you've been afraid to. Because you've been holding on to control so hard that your knuckles are white and the muscles in your hands are fatigued. Pray it now.

Perhaps you've been exploring the Christian faith, but haven't yet asked Jesus to be your Guide along the Way. Now is the time. It can be a simple prayer like this that opens for you the door of salvation: "Jesus, I sense you've been there waiting for me. You know all about me – you always have. And now you are calling to me, 'Follow me.' My answer is, Yes, I will follow you. Please forgive me of my sins, cleanse my heart and

---

[32] "Everlasting" is *'ôlām*, "forever, ever, everlasting, evermore, perpetual, old, ancient," pointing to what is hidden in the distant future or in the distant past (Allan A. MacRae, *'lm*, TWOT #1631a).

[33] Herbert Wolf, *dārak*, TWOT #453a.

[34] *Nāḥā*, TWOT #1314.

motives, and embrace me in your protection and care. I give myself to you now. In the holy name of Jesus, I pray. Amen."

We've been studying prayer, dear friends. and now is the time to put it into practice. Will you begin to pray David's prayer of surrender as your own heart's cry?

"Search me, O God, and know my heart;
test me and know my anxious thoughts.
See if there is any offensive way in me,
and lead me in the way everlasting." (Psalm 139:23-24)

Q4. (Psalm 139:23-24) Why is this prayer of surrender to God so difficult to pray? When was the first time you prayed this kind of prayer to God? What was the result? Can a person be a genuine disciple without praying this kind of prayer?
http://www.joyfulheart.com/forums/index.php?act=ST&f=89&t=369

Prayer

O Lord, do that intense searching in me afresh. I give you full permission – as if you needed it. Refine me and make me the person you've wanted me to be before I ever took a breath. Complete your dream for me in my life and heart. And lead me in your Way, now and forever. In Jesus' name, I pray. Amen.

Key Verses

This passage has not just one or two key verses, but several. I encourage you to commit them to memory:

"If I say, 'Surely the darkness will hide me
and the light become night around me,'
even the darkness will not be dark to you;
the night will shine like the day,
for darkness is as light to you." (Psalm 139:11-12)

"For you created my inmost being;
you knit me together in my mother's womb.
I praise you because I am fearfully and wonderfully made;
your works are wonderful, I know that full well.
My frame was not hidden from you when I was made in the secret place.
When I was woven together in the depths of the earth,
your eyes saw my unformed body.
All the days ordained for me

were written in your book
before one of them came to be." (Psalm 139:13-16)

"Search me, O God, and know my heart;
test me and know my anxious thoughts.
See if there is any offensive way in me,
and lead me in the way everlasting." (Psalm 139:23-24)

7. Hezekiah's Petitions for Deliverance and Healing (2 Kings 19:14-19; 20:1-7)

Imagine the scene. The Assyrian army, the most powerful military force on earth, is ravaging the countryside a few miles away, threatening weaker cities into submission and destroying the rest, carting away their riches and levying a burdensome annual tax that bleeds the nation even more. Hundreds of thousands of enemy soldiers are within a two or three days march.

Hezekiah spread the letter before the Lord (2 Kings 19:14), woodcut from illustrated German Bible, by R.S., unknown artist.

You are Hezekiah, king of Judah, caught in the middle. Your capital is the fortress city of Jerusalem, high on the mountain chain that bisects Palestine. Stress is your daily companion. One report follows another of a city breached and burned, another cowed into submission. None is able to stand before the Assyrian army.

Your people quail in fear, many calling for you to submit to Assyrians. "Resistance is hopeless," they cry. "You'll get us all killed." Yet you are a believer in Yahweh, the true God. "He will save us," you tell your people. Times couldn't be more desperate, more bleak, more filled with violence. How do you pray in a time like this? What do you say to God?

Hezekiah the King

Judah was a relatively small country caught between the nutcracker of Assyria (present-day Iraq) and the Egyptians, who encouraged rebellion against Assyria. While the dating and order of events of this time period are confusing,[1] here is the gist of what is going on.

---

[1] E.J. Young discusses the various problems of dating and reconciling accounts in a long and detailed appendix (Edward J. Young, *The Book of Isaiah* (Eerdmans, 1969), Vol. 2, Appendix 1, pp. 540-555). The

The Assyrians controlled the countries to the north and west of Judah. Previous Assyrian kings had attacked the Northern Kingdom of Samaria – Tiglath Pileser III (745-727 BC), Shalmanezer V (727-722), and Sargon II (722-705). Samaria finally fell in 722 BC and the Northern Kingdom ceased to exist (2 Kings 17:3-6; 18:9-12). The Assyrian kings also conquered Philistine cities west of Judah and imposed a tribute upon Hezekiah's father.

Hezekiah ascended the throne as King of Judah and began his sole reign at age 25 in 716/15, reigning 29 years until his death in 687. He was one of Judah's only "righteous and just" kings, bringing about a number of reforms during his reign. He was known as one who "trusted in the Lord" (18:5), "held fast" and followed him (18:6), with the result that the Lord was with him (18:7) and gave him victory (18:8). Some of his religious reforms included:

- Calling a national Passover (2 Chronicles 29:5-11).
- Reopening the temple, which had been closed by his father, repairing it, and reorganizing its services, priests, and Levites (2 Chronicles 31:11-21).
- Opposing idol worship (2 Chronicles 30:14), toppling the hilltop "high places" where Baal was worshipped, smashing sacred stones, cutting down Asherah poles, and destroying Moses' bronze snake that had become an object of worship (2 Kings 18:4).

When Sargon II conquered the Philistine city of Ashdod in 711, Hezekiah avoided war. But when Assyrian troops departed, Hezekiah began to assert independence. "He rebelled against the king of Assyria and did not serve him" (1 Kings 18:7). He stopped paying tribute and expanded Judah's influence by attacking Philistine cities as far as Gaza that were allies of Assyria (18:8). Hezekiah was one of the chief ringleaders in a rebellion against Assyria.

In 701 BC, another Assyrian king Sennacherib (705-681) led a massive military force into the area to put down the rebels, counteract Egyptian threats, and reassert Assyria's dominance. Anticipating conflict with Assyria, Hezekiah had taken a number of steps:

- Tunneling a shaft through 1,748 feet of solid rock to supply water to the city in time of siege (2 Kings 20:20).
- Stopping up springs around Jerusalem that could supply water to an attacking
- Assyrian army (2 Chronicles 32:1-4).

---

period is also discussed in Donald J. Wiseman, *1 & 2 Kings: An Introduction and Commentary* (Tyndale Old Testament Commentaries; InterVarsity Press, 1993), pp. 271-285; and Samuel J. Schultz, "Hezekiah," ISBE 2:703-705.

- Extending and strengthening the wall of Jerusalem (2 Chronicles 32:5a).
- Increasing the production of shields and weapons (2 Chronicles 32:5b).
- Organizing combat forces (2 Chronicles 32:6)

The Assyrian armies crushed the rebels in Phoenicia and the Philistine coastal cities. Then they turned inland. They couldn't allow Judah's rebellious tendencies to weaken their dominance of the area, which they needed to control as a buffer against their archenemy Egypt. Judah's walled cities were conquered and many of its villages given as punishment and political favors to loyal vassals in Philistia. Finally, Jerusalem was besieged and Hezekiah was forced to admit his rebellion and pay a huge tribute to lift the siege. Assyrian records from Sennacherib gloat over the victory:

> "As to Hezekiah the Jew, he did not submit to my yoke. I laid siege to 46 of his strong cities, walled forts, and to the countless small villages in their vicinity and conquered them.... Himself I made a prisoner in Jerusalem, his royal residence, like a bird in a cage. I surrounded him with earthwork...."[2]

The scripture records the humiliating conclusion:

> "So Hezekiah king of Judah sent this message to the king of Assyria at Lachish: 'I have done wrong. Withdraw from me, and I will pay whatever you demand of me.' The king of Assyria exacted from Hezekiah king of Judah three hundred talents of silver and thirty talents of gold. So Hezekiah gave him all the silver that was found in the temple of the LORD and in the treasuries of the royal palace. At this time Hezekiah king of Judah stripped off the gold with which he had covered the doors and doorposts of the temple of the LORD, and gave it to the king of Assyria." (2 Kings 18:14-15).

Records of Sennacherib's military campaigns are incised on this 6-sided baked clay prism in tiny cuneiform script. In the Museum of the Oriental Institute, University of Chicago.

The Assyrians felt after this that they had made a

---

[2] Quoted from the Prism of Sennacherib, in James B. Pritchard (ed.), *The Ancient Near East: An Anthology of Texts and Pictures* (Princeton University Press/Oxford University Press, 1958), "Sennacherib (704-681 BC): The Siege of Jerusalem," pp. 199-201 (corresponds to ANET 287-288).

tactical error leaving Jerusalem unconquered. Sennacherib, encamped at Lachish a few miles south, sent his field commander ("Rabshakeh," KJV, NRSV) with a large army to Jerusalem again. He threatened and belittled Hezekiah and insulted Yahweh himself:

> "Do not listen to Hezekiah, for he is misleading you when he says, 'The LORD will deliver us.' ... Who of all the gods of these countries has been able to save his land from me? How then can the LORD deliver Jerusalem from my hand?" (2 Kings 18:32, 35)

The prophet Isaiah reassured Hezekiah, and the Assyrian army withdrew to fight the Egyptians (2 Kings 19:9). Then a letter came to Hezekiah demanding that he surrender Jerusalem. We'll pause now and consider Hezekiah's prayer in verses 14-19.

The Battle Is the Lord's (19:14-16)

> "And Hezekiah received the letter of the hand of the messengers, and read it: and Hezekiah went up into the house of the LORD, and spread it before the LORD.... Give ear, O Lord, and hear; open your eyes, O LORD, and see; listen to the words Sennacherib has sent to insult the living God." (19:14, 16)

When Hezekiah receives the letter, he brings it before the Lord and spreads it out for God to read. He reads it to God and observes that the insult is to the living God far more than it is to Hezekiah himself. This is God's insult and demand's God's response.

Earlier, Hezekiah had encouraged the people with his own confidence in the greatness of the power of the unseen God:

> "Do not be afraid or discouraged
> because of the king of Assyria
> and the vast army with him,
> for **there is a greater power with us
> than with him**.
> With him is only the arm of flesh,

Detail of Sennacherib on his throne about 701 BC. From wall relief, "Capitulation of Lachish in Palestine," Southwest Palace of Sennacherib, Nineveh.

but with us is **the Lord our God
to help us and to fight our battles.**" (2 Chronicles 32:7b-8a)

It sounds much like Elisha's assurance to his servant at the siege of Dothan, where they are surrounded by the horses and chariots of fire of the Lord's army:

"Don't be afraid... Those who are with us are more than those who are with them" (2 Kings 6:16).

In the New Testament, John writes:

"The one who is in you is greater than the one who is in the world." (1 John 4:4)

It is vital to understand that Hezekiah is bringing God's problem to God, rather than trying to solve it himself. The principle is: "The Battle Is the Lord's!" This is not an excuse to do nothing. Hezekiah has made all the military preparations he can, but now is the time to look to the Lord. Consider:

David to Goliath and the Philistines:

"All those gathered here will know
that it is not by sword or spear that the Lord saves;
for **the battle is the Lord's,**
and he will give all of you into our hands." (1 Samuel 17:47)

Jahaziel:

"Listen, King Jehoshaphat and all who live in Judah and Jerusalem!
This is what the Lord says to you:
'Do not be afraid or discouraged because of this vast army.
For **the battle is not yours, but God's.**'" (2 Chronicles 20:14)

Zechariah:

"This is the word of the Lord to Zerubbabel:
'Not by might nor by power, but by my Spirit,'
says the Lord Almighty." (Zechariah 4:6)

Think of the pressure we take upon ourselves when we try to be the general in God's battles. We get discouraged. We give up. We fold our tents and go home. We can't handle it. But when we actually believe that the battle is the Lord's to fight, then we let *him* be the general and just follow his orders. Yes, we're under the stress of battle, but not the stress of trying to play God.

Q1. (19:14) What is the significance of Hezekiah spreading out the enemy's message before the Lord? What is the underlying principle illustrated here? How can we apply this principle to our own lives? What happens when we don't apply this principle?
http://www.joyfulheart.com/forums/index.php?act=ST&f=88&t=362

Hezekiah's Vision of Yahweh (19:15)

Hezekiah brings the letter before the Lord and begins his prayer.

"O LORD, God of Israel, enthroned between the cherubim,
you alone are God over all the kingdoms of the earth.
You have made heaven and earth." (19:15)

This corresponds to the magnificent opening of the Lord's Prayer,

"Our Father, who art in heaven,
hallowed be thy name."

Hezekiah begins his prayer with an awesome vision of who God really is.

"LORD" is the Hebrew personal, specific name of God, pronounced "YAW-whey." The Jews felt that the name of the Lord was too holy to even pronounce, and substituted for it when reading or speaking the word *Adonai*, "lord." In most English Bibles when you see LORD in small caps it indicates Yahweh. Hezekiah calls his God by name.

"God of Israel." Israel is the name God gave to Jacob (Genesis 32:28) and is applied to the nation. In the period of the divided kingdom, Israel was generally used to designate the Northern Kingdom as opposed to Judah, the Southern Kingdom. It is significant that Hezekiah uses this term, shortly after the fall of the Northern Kingdom, to refer to the remaining remnant of God's people.

"Enthroned between the cherubim." "Enthroned" (NIV, NRSV) and "dwellest" (KJV) is the common verb *yāshab*, "sit, remain, dwell." Cherubim is the plural of *kᵉrûb*, "angelic beings who are represented as part human, part animal."[3] The reference here is to the pair of cherubs facing each other whose wings overshadow the cover of the ark of the covenant (Exodus 25:20). The ark of the covenant typified the throne of God in the Holy of Holies – the cover or "mercy seat" as his dwelling place and the cherubim serving as guardians on each side. Hezekiah prays to Yahweh whom he sees as enthroned between the cherubim, in a much higher place than any earthly king. His vision of God drives his own faith in Yahweh's power.

[3] R. Laird Harris, *kerûb*, TWOT #1036.

"You alone are God over all the kingdoms of the earth." Hezekiah is a monotheist, a believer in one God. And he asserts that God's reign extends over and encompasses every human kingdom on earth, including the Assyrian empire.

"You have made heaven and earth." Hezekiah sees no limitation to God's power, since he made heaven and earth and can control anything within them. In 1952, J.B. Phillips wrote *Your God Is Too Small.*[4] The title says it all. If our own vision of God is small, we'll never ask of him great things. Hezekiah's prayer springs from his faith in the God of creation.

A Prayer for Deliverance (19:15-19)

Look at his prayer one more time:

> "O LORD, God of Israel, enthroned between the cherubim, you alone are God over all the kingdoms of the earth. You have made heaven and earth. Give ear, O Lord, and hear; open your eyes, O LORD, and see; listen to the words Sennacherib has sent to insult the living God.

> It is true, O LORD, that the Assyrian kings have laid waste these nations and their lands. They have thrown their gods into the fire and destroyed them, for they were not gods but only wood and stone, fashioned by men's hands.

> Now, O LORD our God, deliver us from his hand, so that all kingdoms on earth may know that you alone, O LORD, are God." (19:15-19)

The actual petition is quite brief: "Deliver us from his hand!" The basis of Hezekiah's appeal is that God be seen by the nations as the only true God.

Q2. (19:15) How do the first two sentences of Hezekiah's prayer (verse 15) correspond to the first sentence of the Lord's Prayer? How are they important to faith? How are they important to God answering the prayer?
http://www.joyfulheart.com/forums/index.php?act=ST&f=88&t=363

The Answer to Prayer (19:20, 35-37)

The answer was not long in coming through Isaiah the prophet:

> "This is what the LORD, the God of Israel, says:
> I have heard your prayer concerning Sennacherib king of Assyria." (19:20)

After a poetic oracle or prophecy, the narrator recounts:

[4] J.B. Phillips, *Your God Is Too Small* (1952; Touchstone, reprint 1997)

"That night the angel of the LORD went out and put to death a hundred and eighty-five thousand men in the Assyrian camp. When the people got up the next morning – there were all the dead bodies! So Sennacherib king of Assyria broke camp and withdrew. He returned to Nineveh and stayed there.

"One day, while he was worshiping in the temple of his god Nisroch, his sons Adrammelech and Sharezer cut him down with the sword, and they escaped to the land of Ararat. And Esarhaddon his son succeeded him as king." (19:35- 37)

Hezekiah's Illness (2 Kings 20:1)

God answered Hezekiah's prayer, but then another crisis loomed.

"In those days Hezekiah became ill and was at the point of death. The prophet Isaiah son of Amoz went to him and said, 'This is what the LORD says: Put your house in order, because you are going to die; you will not recover.'" (20:1)

The timing of the illness, "in those days," can't be determined exactly,[5] but it may well have taken place around 701 BC at the time of Sennacharib's campaign. From God's response to Hezekiah's prayer through the Prophet Isaiah (20:6b), it sounds like Sennacharib's presence was still threatening Jerusalem at this time. What a time to fall ill and die! What a difficult time this would have been to leave his country leaderless!

Hezekiah mortal illness involved a boil (20:7), Hebrew *shehîn*, "boil, enflamed spot."[6] This may have been a furuncle or carbuncle, the latter being "a more extensive inflammation of the skin, usually attended by a lowering of bodily resistance, and it can prove fatal."[7] To us, most infections are easily cured with antibiotics, but in those days, a serious infection could bring death.

You may think it cruel to tell Hezekiah to "Put your house in order," but it was really a kindness. It is likely that he had no clear successor at that point. If this took place in 701, it was before his son Manasseh was born. Hezekiah needed to name a successor so leadership would pass to another at his death without palace intrigues and unnecessary disruption to the kingdom.

God's Word and Human Response (20:1b)

The Lord said, "You will die; you will not recover" (20:1b), but that didn't happen. Why? When we considered Moses' intercession in Exodus 32, we discussed the interplay between God's judgment and human response. Without any change in the situation,

---

[5] Young, *Isaiah* 2:509.
[6] Elmer A. Martens, *shhn*, TWOT #2364a.
[7] Alexander Macalister and Roland K. Harrison, "Boil," ISBE 1:532.

God's word stands. But with a different human response, the outcome can be different, though all within the boundaries of God's will. Vitringa, an eighteenth century Dutch scholar, put it this way:

> "According to natural causes [Hezekiah] would have to die, unless with His aid God should intervene beyond the ordinary. God, however, had decided not to intervene, unless at the supplication of the king and the trials of his faith and hope. Moreover, in cases of this kind (Genesis 20:3) the condition is not expressed, in order that God may call it forth as voluntary."[8]

But Hezekiah *did* respond in prayer and faith, and God changed his mind. Let's examine Hezekiah's short prayer.

Hezekiah's Weeping (20:2-3)

> "Hezekiah turned his face to the wall and prayed to the Lord, 'Remember, O LORD, how I have walked before you faithfully and with wholehearted devotion and have done what is good in your eyes.' And Hezekiah wept bitterly." (20:2-3)

The common English translations of the adjective describing Hezekiah's weeping do us a disservice. "Bitterly" (NIV, NRSV) and "sore" (KJV) suggest a wrong attitude on Hezekiah's part where the text doesn't imply any. The adjective is *gādōl*, "great," indicating "many" in number and other intensified concepts like "loudness" in sound, being old in years," etc.[9] A good translation in this context is "profusely." Hezekiah wept a lot; he wept profusely.

What kind of a baby is Hezekiah? Isn't it interesting how we westerners tend to see tears as a sign of weakness in a man? "Real men don't cry," is the way we train our sons. It's part of the macho exterior that men try to project. But in Hezekiah's culture, men were able to admit and express their emotions openly. It was no shame to cry when under stress.

Was Hezekiah terrified of death? Was he a faithless whiner? Certainly he did not look forward to death with the same longing as Paul, who saw it as "far better" (Philippians 1:23). But it is unfair to judge him by *our* knowledge this side of the cross. Hezekiah didn't know about eternal life in the presence of God; it was a later revelation.

His tears probably represent more than a fear of death. As mentioned above, it is likely that he had no heir yet, no one to carry on the line of Davidic kings promised centuries before that would culminate in a Messiah (2 Samuel 7:11-16). Hezekiah was a

---

[8] Translated and cited by Young, *Isaiah* 2:509, fn. 3, from Campegius Vitringa, *Commentarius in librum propheticum Jesaie* (Leeuwarden, 1714-1720), commenting on Isaiah 38.
[9] Elmer B. Smick, *gādal*, TWOT #315d.

godly man who hoped in God. Young suggests: "Hezekiah could well be facing the same temptation that came to Abraham when he was commanded to offer up his son (Genesis 22:1)"[10] – that is, the conflict of God's promise concerning his offspring with God's command that seemed to conflict with the promise.

Turning His Face to the Wall (20:2)

What does it mean, "Hezekiah turned his face to the wall and prayed to the Lord...."? Is this a childish, petulant response to an unwelcome word from God's prophet? I don't think so.

He is in his own bedroom, probably hovered over by various counselors, officers, and physicians who are concerned at the impending death of this strong and godly king. To be alone with God that he might pray with some privacy and without interruption, he turns to the wall. God has been his help in crisis many times. He turns to God now in earnest and heartfelt prayer. His tears are tears of emotion and struggle. You've been there. You know. Hezekiah is a human, weakened by illness, facing the heavy responsibilities of defending his nation against its enemies. In addition, now he faces death and the burden of succession.

Hezekiah's Petition (20:2-3)

"Prayed" is *pālal*, "intervene, interpose, pray," the most common Hebrew root for prayer and praying, the verb occurring 84 times in the Old Testament. Though the exact derivation of the root is a matter of conjecture, both the verb and the noun (*tᵉpillâ*, 20:5) refer most often to intercessory prayer.[11] Here he petitions God strongly for his own life, but because of his position and responsibility, he also prays for his nation's uncertain future – under military pressure, leaderless, and without a successor that can inspire national unity and resistance.

His prayer seems short, but he knows God well by this time in his life, and in its shortness and abbreviation of expression much is implied:

"Remember, O LORD, how I have walked before you faithfully and with wholehearted devotion and have done what is good in your eyes." (20:3)

You may think it naive of Hezekiah to appeal to God on the basis of his own righteousness. After all, everyone sins. But his righteousness is not only his own judgment, but the judgment of the inspired writer of Kings, who tells us:

---

[10] Young, *Isaiah* 2:510.
[11] Victor P. Hamilton, *pālal*, TWOT #1776.

"He did what was right in the eyes of the Lord...." (2 Kings 18:1)

"Hezekiah trusted in the Lord, the God of Israel. There was no one like him among all the kings of Judah, either before him or after him. He held fast to the Lord and did not cease to follow him; he kept the commands the Lord had given Moses. And the Lord was with him; he was successful in whatever he undertook." (2 Kings 18:5-7a)

Why does Hezekiah say what he does? I believe he is appealing to God's promises to David concerning his son Solomon and Solomon's offspring:

"When he does wrong, I will punish him with the rod of men, with floggings inflicted by men. But my love will never be taken away from him, as I took it away from Saul, whom I removed from before you. **Your house and your kingdom will endure forever before me; your throne will be established forever.**" (2 Samuel 7:14-16)

God promised an unbroken line of David's sons upon the throne. Hezekiah is also appealing to God's promises for offspring and for a long life to those who walk uprightly before him:

"Honor your father and your mother,
so that **you may live long in the land**
the Lord your God is giving you." (Exodus 20:12)

"Keep his decrees and commands, which I am giving you today, so that **it may go well with you and your children after you and that you may live long in the land** the Lord your God gives you for all time." (Deuteronomy 4:40)

"Do not eat [blood], so that **it may go well with you and your children after you**, because you will be doing what is right in the eyes of the Lord." (Deuteronomy 12:25)

Hezekiah, I am sure, had not reached sinless perfection, but he had been careful (unlike his father) to live a godly, righteous, and faithful life before the Lord. He had been zealous for the Lord, in the face of much pressure and criticism from idolaters. He had encouraged the people with confidence and trust in God when threatened by his enemies. Hezekiah not only *talked* about a righteous life. He *lived* it! He walked the walk!

Q3. Why is Hezekiah's healing important for his nation? How did it relate to God's promises to David?

http://www.joyfulheart.com/forums/index.php?act=ST&f=88&t=364

God's Immediate Answer (20:4-7)

Hezekiah appealed to God's promises for an heir and for long life for those who live a righteous life. God heard and answered quickly:

> "Before Isaiah had left the middle court, the word of the LORD came to him: 'Go back and tell Hezekiah, the leader of my people, "This is what the LORD, the God of your father David, says: I have heard your prayer ($t^e pill\hat{a}$) and seen your tears; I will heal you. On the third day from now you will go up to the temple of the LORD. I will add fifteen years to your life. And I will deliver you and this city from the hand of the king of Assyria. I will defend this city for my sake and for the sake of my servant David."'" (20:4-6)

Wow! God's answer is both amazing and wonderful. A saint of God prays and immediately God both changes his mind and sends alternate instructions to his prophet. A few minutes after Hezekiah prays, Isaiah returns to his bedroom. Hezekiah is still lying on his side facing the wall. Isaiah says: "Hezekiah, this is what the LORD, the God of your father David, says...." Hezekiah turns over with wonder and joy on his face.

> "Then Isaiah said, 'Prepare a poultice of figs.' They did so and applied it to the boil, and he recovered." (20:7)

According to Pliny, figs were used for the cure of ulcers.[12] Did the poultice of figs cure Hezekiah? It was probably instrumental, but only because God enabled it. Prior to this, Hezekiah was about to die and no figs would have helped. It is God who turned the situation around! Within three days Hezekiah would be strong enough to get out of bed and to go up to the temple (verse 6d).

Did Hezekiah Ask Wrongly?

I've heard people accuse Hezekiah of selfishness in his prayer for healing. The result of his prayer, this argument contends, is the birth of Manasseh, the worst king Judah had ever seen. If Hezekiah hadn't asked for healing, Manasseh would never have been born. Be careful what you pray for! That argument is specious and weak. Here's why.

1. The Bible never indicates that requesting prayer for healing is selfish. Where in the Bible do you find such a preposterous suggestion? (James 5:14-15; Matthew 10:7; 12:15; etc.)

2. Judah had a long history of bad kings before and after Hezekiah. Hezekiah isn't responsible for Manesseh's sins any more than God is.

---

[12] Pliny, *Hist. Nat.* 23.7.122.

3. Without Manasseh, we wouldn't have had Josiah the boy king who brought about great reforms.

4. Beyond seeking to pray within the boundaries of what we know to be God's will, the dictum of "Be careful what you pray for," is useless. No one can see the future but God. No one could have predicted Manasseh's wickedness except God himself.

5. We pray to a Father who gives us what is good for us, not what is bad for us (Matthew 7:7-11). We can trust our prayers to a loving Father, who knows better that we do.

6. God chose to answer Hezekiah's prayer and to bless him during his lifetime. Let's not confuse this by second-guessing.

Why Did God Grant Hezekiah's Prayer?

From God's response through Isaiah we get some hints to the reasons why God seems to have responded to Hezekiah's prayer, though we can't read God's mind:

1. **Hezekiah prayed**. If he hadn't asked, God would have continued with the plan announced by Isaiah – an early death. James says, "You do not have, because you do not ask God...." (James 4:2b).

2. **Promises made to David** centuries before. The Lord identifies himself as "the God of your father David..." (verse 5b) and says he will defend the city "for the sake of my servant David" (verse 6b).

3. **Respect for Hezekiah's leadership role**. "Hezekiah, the leader of my people" (verse 5a).

4. **Concern for Jerusalem's welfare**. I will deliver you and this city from the hand of the king of Assyria. I will defend this city...." (verse 6).

5. **Honor for Hezekiah's upright life**. "I have heard your prayer," indicates that he has heard Hezekiah's implied prayer and honored the basis on which he made it, an upright life.

6. **Love for Hezekiah**. "I have heard your prayer and seen your tears" (verse 5c). Hezekiah loves God and God loves Hezekiah. The Father has seen his child's tears and responded.

You, dear friend, are also loved by God. He has redeemed you by the blood of Jesus, which cannot be valued because it is so costly. He has made promises to you. He has encouraged you to pray to him. You may not be a king, but you have influence important to the kingdom. I encourage you to pray.

The Prayer of a Righteous Man or Woman

I also encourage you to consider personal holiness. Sometimes God answers the prayers of rank sinners and backslidden Christians. But his ear is particularly open to his children who seek to be obedient to him.

Consider your own children's petitions. When your child is being openly rebellious, are you quick to respond to his demands? No, you withhold everything except the necessities so your actions aren't construed as rewarding disobedience. But when your child is compliant and obedient – and asks for something special – you think twice about saying no. You want to say yes. And if it won't hurt him, you'll often give it to him.

This doesn't mean you must be sinless to get your prayers answered. Hezekiah wasn't sinless (2 Chronicles 32:26). He had made mistakes, wrong decisions, and had moments that reflect a weakness of faith. But Hezekiah made an honest attempt to follow God in his life and repented when he was convicted of his sin. God honored this with blessing, success, and answered prayer.

In no way do I want to imply that God owes us anything, that salvation is by works rather than grace. This isn't a works-righteousness mentality. It's just good heavenly parenting. All God's gifts are by grace – his own favor towards us, which is neither earned nor deserved.

But God *does* honor the prayers of the upright over those of the backslidden. James teaches us:

"The prayer of a *righteous man* is powerful and effective" (James 5:16b).

Q4. (20:3) What is the basis on which Hezekiah asks for healing? Why is personal righteousness and holiness important in getting your prayers answered? How can unrighteousness prevent answered prayer if all gifts from God are by grace anyway?
http://www.joyfulheart.com/forums/index.php?act=ST&f=88&t=365

The Bottom Line

What do I learn from Hezekiah's example of a prayer that God will answer? God's heart is open to the prayer of his child seeking to live a faithful, upright, righteous life.

Since God has less need for discipline, he has greater freedom to grant us answers to our prayers without hurting us.

Can you pray Hezekiah's simple prayer? "Remember, O LORD, how I have walked before you faithfully and with wholehearted devotion and have done what is good in your eyes." I hope so.

Prayer

Father, help us to move from being unruly children to the place where you don't need to discipline us so much. Help us to be like your servant Hezekiah, who trusted in you and your promises with all his heart, and wasn't afraid to ask you for what he needed. Help us grow. In Jesus' name, we pray. Amen.

Key Verses

"And Hezekiah prayed to the LORD: 'O LORD, God of Israel, enthroned between the cherubim, you alone are God over all the kingdoms of the earth. You have made heaven and earth. Give ear, O Lord, and hear; open your eyes, O LORD, and see; listen to the words Sennacherib has sent to insult the living God.'" (2 Kings 19:15-16)

"Hezekiah turned his face to the wall and prayed to the Lord, 'Remember, O LORD, how I have walked before you faithfully and with wholehearted devotion and have done what is good in your eyes.'" (2 Kings 20:2-3)

8. Daniel's Confession on Behalf of His People (Daniel 9:1-19)

We want to learn prayer from someone who knows prayer – who prays and God answers. Our mentor for this lesson is the prophet Daniel. Daniel was considered one of the most righteous men in history – placed by God alongside Noah and Job (Ezekiel 14:14-20). He was punished for praying, persisted, was thrown to the lions, and conquered. One of his prayers was resisted by the "prince of Persia," but God sent the answer nonetheless (Daniel 10:12-13). For nearly 60 years he served at the top rungs of a pagan government, serving three different kings without compromising his relationship to God. And in the passage we are studying today he acts as intercessor for the entire people of Israel.

Sir Edward Poynter (English neoclassical painter, 1836-1919), Daniel's Prayer (1865), from illustrations for *Dalziel's Bible Gallery*. Relief print on paper, 190 x 175 mm, Tate Collection.

Daniel's Life

Let's start from the beginning. The Northern Kingdom had fallen to Assyria in 722 BC. Now the Southern Kingdom of Judah had ended, too, conquered in 605 BC and finally destroyed by the armies of Babylon in 587 BC. As a young man Daniel was exiled or deported in 605

BC along with many other youths from royal or noble families to be trained to serve in the king's palace in Babylon. In Babylon, Daniel was given the name Belteshazzar ("protect his life") and underwent three years of specialized education and training (1:5). Because the food supplied was offensive to Jewish dietary laws, he found favor with his superiors to change his diet and that of his comrades.

In about 602, he entered the service of Nebuchadnezzar, king of Babylon (reigned 605-562 BC, 1:19) as a "wise man" (2:12). He was not only well-educated. God had supernaturally gifted him with spiritual wisdom and insight as a prophet (1:17). When Daniel interpreted a dream for Nebuchadnezzar,

> "The king placed Daniel in a high position and lavished many gifts on him. He made him ruler over the entire province of Babylon and placed him in charge of all its wise men" (2:48), "chief of the magicians" (Daniel 4:9).

After Nebuchadnezzar died in 562 BC, Nabonidus reigned as the last of the Neo-Babylonian kings (556-539 BC). His son Belshazzar served as co-regent with him (c. 553-539 BC). Daniel interprets for Belshazzar the Dream of the Four Beasts (chapter 7) and has a Vision of a Ram and a Goat (chapter 8). Finally, Daniel delivers God's word to Belshazzar and interprets an inscription written by the hand of God: "Mene, mene, tekel, parsin." That night the city of Babylon was defeated by Darius the Mede (5:25-31), who is either (1) Gubaru, an Assyrian governor of Babylon or (2) is another name for the Persian king Cyrus II ("the Great," reigned 559-530 BC).[1] The world empire of Babylon had fallen and the Persian empire was on the rise.

But Daniel, now probably 80 to 85 years old, found favor in the eyes of Darius, who appointed him as one of three administrators over Babylon. He was set to become chief administrator, but to have a Jew in such a high position made the others jealous. They tricked Darius into passing a law making it illegal to pray to any god or man except Darius himself (6:7-9).

> "Now when Daniel learned that the decree had been published, he went home to his upstairs room where the windows opened toward Jerusalem. Three times a day he got down on his knees and prayed, giving thanks to his God, just as he had done before. Then these men went as a group and found Daniel praying and asking God for help." (6:10-11)

---

[1] David J.A. Clines, "Darius," ISBE 1:867-868. David J.A. Clines, "Cyrus," ISBE 1:845-849. Joyce G. Baldwin, *Daniel: An Introduction and Commentary* (Tyndale Old Testament Commentaries; InterVarsity Press, 1978), pp. 23-28, 163. This Darius is to be distinguished from Darius Hystaspes who came to the throne in 522.

They reported him and as a result old, faithful Daniel is thrown into the lion's den, much to Darius' chagrin. In the morning he calls out to Daniel, hoping he is alive. Daniel answers:

Briton Rivière (British painter, 1840-1920), "Daniel's Answer to the King" (1890), oil on canvas, 74x47-7/16 inches, Manchester Art Gallery, UK.

> "O king, live forever! My God sent his angel, and he shut the mouths of the lions. They have not hurt me, because I was found innocent in his sight. Nor have I ever done any wrong before you, O king." (6:21-22)

God is glorified, Daniel's enemies became lion fodder instead of him, and

> "Daniel prospered during the reign of Darius and [margin *"that is"*] the reign of Cyrus the Persian." (NIV, 6:28)

In Darius' first year, Daniel prays the prayer of confession (chapter 9) that we are studying in this lesson. In Cyrus' third year he has visions of a Man (chapter 10), the Kings of the South and the North (chapter 11), the King Who Exalts Himself (11:36-45), and more visions of the end times (chapter 12). Daniel died in Babylon, never to return to his homeland. But his intercession to God made it possible for many of his people to return to Jerusalem and rebuild the temple.

70 Years Are Completed (9:1-3)

We begin our study today with a clear historical reference point, 539 BC:

> "In the first year of Darius son of Xerxes (a Mede by descent), who was made ruler over the Babylonian kingdom – in the first year of his reign, I, Daniel, understood from the Scriptures, according to the word of the LORD given to Jeremiah the prophet, that the desolation[2] of Jerusalem would last seventy years." (9:1-3)

---

[2] "Desolation" (NIV, KJV) or "devastation" (NRSV) is *horbâ*, "waste or desolate places, ruins" from the verb *ḥārēb* "to be desolate, be dry, be in ruins, lay waste" (Edwin Yamauchi, *ḥārēb*, TWOT #731d).

As mentioned above, we're not precisely sure of the identity of this Darius – he may have been Cyrus himself. In any case he began his reign over the Babylonian kingdom when the Medes and the Persians conquered Babylon in 539 BC.

Prior to this, Daniel has been reading and pondering the Scriptures (*sēper*, "writing, book"),[3] in this case, the prophecy of Jeremiah, who had prophesied 66 years previously in 605 BC.

> "'This whole country will become a desolate wasteland, and these nations will serve the king of Babylon seventy years. But when the seventy years are fulfilled, I will punish the king of Babylon and his nation, the land of the Babylonians, for their guilt,' declares the LORD, 'and will make it desolate forever.'" (Jeremiah 25:11-12; see also Jeremiah 29:10; 2 Chronicles 36:20-21 and Zechariah 1:12)

Daniel realizes that this 70 years is just about completed, that the prophecy is just about to be fulfilled. This 70 years is a round figure, perhaps a normal lifespan, but probably should be figured from the fourth year of Jehoiakim (605 BC) to the start of the return under Cyrus' regime, 536 BC or thereabouts.[4]

Q1. (9:1-3) What encourages Daniel to seek God for the forgiveness and restoration of Israel to its homeland? What trait on Daniel's part brings this encouragement to pass?

http://www.joyfulheart.com/forums/index.php?act=ST&f=90&t=370

Confession of Israel's Sins (9:3-4a)

Because Daniel believes God's promises for a return, he begins to pray in earnest for his people, that God would forgive their sin and enable this restoration to take place. He could have been a fatalist and decided that God would take care of all the details, that he needn't be concerned. Instead, he takes it upon himself to pray, to intercede, and to plead with God on the basis of his character.

William Carey (1761-1834), who was to become one of the first Protestant missionaries, one day shared his passion to save the heathen of India with others at a minister's meeting. One arrogant hyper-Calvinist clergyman called out, "Young man, sit down:

---

[3] R.D. Patterson, *sāpar*, TWOT #540a.

[4] Baldwin, *Daniel*, p. 164. R.K. Harrison, *Jeremiah and Lamentations: An Introduction and Commentary* (Tyndale Old Testament Commentaries; InterVarsity Press, 1973), p. 126. John Bright (*Jeremiah* (Anchor Bible 21; Doubleday, 1965, second edition), p. 160, fn. 11) notes that in Zechariah 1:12 this 70 years seems to refer to the interval between the destruction of the temple in 587 and its rebuilding in 520-515. In 2 Chronicles 36:20-23 it is made to refer to the period between 587 and Cyrus' edit in 538.

when God pleases to covert the heathen, He will do it without your aid or mine." Some predestinarians presume that God will work out his will on the earth without using human beings as his instruments or means. But that wasn't Daniel's view. Baldwin observes, "Divine decree or no, the Scriptures never support the idea that God's purpose will be accomplished irrespective of the prayers of his people."[5]

> "So I turned to the Lord God[6] and pleaded with him in prayer and petition, in fasting, and in sackcloth and ashes. I prayed to the LORD my God and confessed...." (9:3-4a)

He "turned" (NIV, NRSV), "gave attention to" (NASB), or literally "set my face" (KJV) to the Lord. This is a Hebrew idiom implying a deliberate determination towards something. We see this Hebrew idiom in the New Testament also, when it says, "When the days drew near for him to be taken up, he set his face to go to Jerusalem" (Luke 9:51; NRSV). The NIV translates it, "Jesus resolutely set out for Jerusalem." Daniel's prayer was no casual thing, but a firm heart's resolve to seek God for his people until an answer came.

The seriousness of the prayer is expressed by the phrase, "in fasting, and in sackcloth and ashes." Fasting was a way to humble oneself before God. Sackcloth was a sign of mourning and with ashes "symbolized the penitence with which Daniel came to represent his people before the Lord."[7]

Three words describe the prayer:

Pleaded. Then he "pleaded" (NIV) "to seek" (KJV), or "to seek an answer" (NRSV). This phrase uses the verb *bāqash*, "to seek, require, desire," which connotes a person's earnest seeking of something or someone which exists or thought to exist."[8]

Prayer. In the phrase "prayer and petition," "prayer" is *tepillâ* (from the root *pālal*, which occurs in verse 4), the most common Hebrew word for prayer, occurring 76 times in the Old Testament.[9]

---

[5] Baldwin, *Daniel*, p. 165.

[6] In verse 3, Daniel refers to Yahweh here by a pair of words *'ādōn*, "lord, master, owner," and *'ĕlōhīm*, the generic word for God. In verse 4 he refers to God as "the LORD my God," literally "Yahweh my God." Yahweh is the name by which God revealed himself to Abraham (Genesis 12) and later Moses (Exodus 3:15), God's specific, unique, given name. I don't find any particular significance here of using one expression or the other, only that Daniel feels free to use them interchangeably.

[7] Baldwin, *Daniel*, p. 165.

[8] A noun from this root, *baqqāshā*, "petition," which occurs seven times in the Old Testament, is a technical term "denoting a petition or request by a subject to a king that he grant a specific desire" (Leonard J. Coppes, *bāqash*, TWOT #276).

[9] Victor P. Hamilton, *pālal*, TWOT #1776a.

Petition. "Petition" (NIV) or "supplication" (KJV, NRSV) is *taḥănûn*. The verb *ḥanan* depicts "a heartfelt response by someone who has something to give to one who has a need," that is, a granting of mercy. The noun *taḥănûn*, carries the idea of "a prayer for grace, supplication," but is less a formal entreaty than the outpourings of a troubled soul (used in parallel to "weepings" in Jeremiah 3:21; 31:9).[10]

The phrase, "... in fasting, and in sackcloth and ashes," depicts his manner of prayer – deliberate and abject humility. Daniel doesn't come to God in boldness to plead a righteous cause. God owes him and his people nothing. He comes asking mercy for a clearly sinful people. He comes humbly. Now the Scripture indicates that he takes two actions: "I prayed to the Lord my God and confessed..." (9:4).

"Prayed" is *pālal*, "to pray," the most common verb for praying, of which we saw the noun form in the previous verse.

"Confessed" (NIV) or "made confession" (NRSV, cf. KJV) is *yādā*, which in various contexts can mean, "confess, praise, give thanks, thank." The primary meaning of this root is "to acknowledge or confess sin, God's character and works, or man's character." It is used in David's personal confession of sin (Psalm 32:5), the confession of all the nation's sins made on the Day of Atonement (Leviticus 16:21), and other great confessions of Israel's sins (Ezra 10:1; Nehemiah 1:6 which we'll study in a future lesson; and Nehemiah 9:2-3).[11]

Q2. (9:3-4a) What is Daniel's demeanor as he prays? How does he prepare? Why is this so important in this case? In what ways might you and I prepare for intercession?
http://www.joyfulheart.com/forums/index.php?act=ST&f=90&t=371

Now we proceed to the content of Daniel's confession.

Acknowledgement of Sin (9:4b-6)

Remember how the Lord's Prayer begins, with a recognition of God's greatness and holiness? Daniel begins:

> "O Lord, the great and awesome God, who keeps his covenant of love with all who love him and obey his commands, we have sinned and done wrong. We have been wicked and have rebelled; we have turned away from your commands and laws. We have not

---

[10] Edwin Yamauchi, *ḥanan*, TWOT #694g.
[11] Ralph H. Alexander, *yādā*, TWOT #847.

listened to your servants the prophets, who spoke in your name to our kings, our princes and our fathers, and to all the people of the land." (9:4-6)

First, he acknowledges Yahweh as "the great and awesome God." "Great" is *gādōl*, which we've seen before, meaning here "great in importance."[12] "Awesome" (NIV, NRSV) or "dreadful" (KJV) is *yārē*, "be afraid, revere," which can refer to the emotion of fear as well as to "reverence or awe."[13]

Next, he acknowledges Yahweh's reputation and character, "who keeps his covenant of love with all who love him and obey his commands" (9:4b). A covenant (*bᵉrit*) is "between nations: a treaty, alliance of friendship." God made a covenant with Israel at Mt. Sinai, "accompanied by signs, sacrifices, and a solemn oath that sealed the relationship with promises of blessing for keeping the covenant and curses for breaking it."[14]

With this pair of words it is referred to as a "covenant of love" (NIV) or "covenant and steadfast love" (NRSV) or "covenant and mercy" (KJV). The second word is "love" (*hesed*), "kindness, lovingkindness, mercy," which we discussed previously. Notice that Daniel is quite aware that the people of Israel don't qualify for mercy under the covenant, since it is a covenant "with all who love him and obey his commands" (9:4b). The Israelites have not kept his commands, but broken them and committed treason by worshipping other gods. Instead of the blessings of the covenant, they face the curses of the covenant. Daniel acknowledges this openly:

"We have sinned and done wrong. We have been wicked and have rebelled; we have turned away from your commands and laws. We have not listened to your servants the prophets, who spoke in your name to our kings, our princes and our fathers, and to all the people of the land." (9:5-6)

We've considered most of these words for sin in Psalm 51 and don't need to rehearse them again. Daniel uses all these synonyms for sin to make clear that he isn't trying to get mercy based on some loophole provided for under a "special definition," as we sometimes excuse ourselves. He flat out declares "We have sinned!" Nor does he hide behind the "We-didn't- know-it-was-wrong" defense. He acknowledges that "We have not listened to your servants the prophets, who spoke in your name..." (9:6a). God isn't at fault. He sent prophets to warn them but they didn't listen. Instead they killed the messengers of God's merciful warning.

---

[12] Elmer B. Smick, *gādal*, TWOT #315c.
[13] Andrew Bowling, *yārē'*, TWOT #907.
[14] Elmer B. Smick, *brh*, TWOT #282a.

Honest confession of our sins must be open, complete, and brutally honest, without prevarication, extenuating circumstances, or excuse. Anything less is unacceptable.

As a parent, have you ever confronted your child with a misdeed and waited for him or her to own up to it? Sometimes you'll hear a full admission, but often you hear lies and excuses. Not until the child is truly sorry will he or she fully confess with repentance and grief. But anything less is unacceptable to a parent intent on shaping the child's conscience and character. Why should we expect God to be less discerning than we?

Daniel Confesses the Sin as His Own (9:5)

One of the strongest lessons to me is the way Daniel places himself squarely in the middle of his nation's sin. He doesn't say, "*They* sinned..." or "Seventy years ago some wicked people sinned...." Instead, he says,

> "*We* have sinned and done wrong. *We* have been wicked and have rebelled" (9:5).

If we are to intercede as Daniel did (as a member of the sinning nation), we must in a sense take that sin upon ourselves. Daniel was a very righteous man who lived without compromise all his life. I am sure he committed personal sins, but by any account he would be classified as a righteous man. He is placed by God alongside Noah and Job (Ezekiel 14:14-20). Yet he prays, "We have sinned...."

It is no accident that half a millennium later, Jesus takes on himself the sins of the world in order to save it.

> "... He poured out his life unto death,
> and was **numbered with the transgressors**.
> For he bore the sin of many,
> and made intercession for the transgressors." (Isaiah 53:12)

> "Christ redeemed us from the curse of the law by **becoming a curse for us**,
> for it is written: 'Cursed is everyone who is hung on a tree.'" (Galatians 3:13)

> "But when the time had fully come,
> God sent his Son, born of a woman,
> **born under law, to redeem those under law**,
> that we might receive the full rights of sons." (Galatians 4:4-5)

> "For Christ died for sins once for all,
> **the righteous for the unrighteous**,
> to bring you to God." (1 Peter 3:18a)

> "... Who, being in very nature God,
> did not consider equality with God something to be grasped, but made himself nothing,
> **taking the very nature of a servant**, being made **in human likeness**.

And being found **in appearance as a man,**
he humbled himself
and became obedient to death—
even death on a cross!" (Philippians 2:6-8)

I don't know fully what this means. But surely it means that intercession is costly. Daniel doesn't take on sin in the sense that Jesus did, bearing other's sins on his body on the cross (1 Peter 2:24). But Daniel is part of a sinful nation in the same way that a member of the human race bears guilt because of Adam's sin (Romans 5:12-21).

This is not some legal fiction for Daniel. His intercession is costly. This 80- to 85-year-old man fasts, he wears sackcloth, he sprinkles ashes on his own head. This is not external. He feels the grief, is overwhelmed with the burden, is humbled before God. He, a righteous man, takes ownership, in a sense, for the sins of others so he can intercede for them. Daniel in his own person fulfills for Israel the condition and promise of 2 Chronicles 7:14:

"If my people, who are called by my name, will humble themselves and pray and seek my face and turn from their wicked ways, then will I hear from heaven and will forgive their sin and will heal their land."

How do you and I ask mercy for a sinful nation of which we are citizens? How do we pray for healing for a church whose spirit has been tarnished by sin and hatred? How do we pray for forgiveness and restoration for a church that has left true doctrine for false? How do we pray? Painfully. Personally. We learn from Jesus and from Daniel.

Q3. (9:5) Since Daniel is such a righteous man in his generation, why does he identify himself with the sins of his people? He didn't commit them. How does this compare to how Jesus sought forgiveness for his people?

http://www.joyfulheart.com/forums/index.php?act=ST&f=90&t=372

Israel's Shame (9:7-11a)

Let's continue considering Daniel's prayer of confession:

"Lord, you are righteous, but this day we are covered with shame – the men of Judah and people of Jerusalem and all Israel, both near and far, in all the countries where you have scattered us because of our unfaithfulness to you.

O Lord, we and our kings, our princes and our fathers are covered with shame because we have sinned against you. The Lord our God is merciful and forgiving, even though we have rebelled against him; we have not obeyed the Lord our God or kept the laws he gave us through his servants the prophets. All Israel has transgressed your law and turned away, refusing to obey you." (9:7-11a)

Daniel contrasts God's righteousness (*sᵉdāqā*) with Israel's shame (*boshnâ*). The word comes from a root that means "to fall into disgrace, normally through failure, either of self or of an object of trust." It contains nuances of "confusion, disillusionment, humiliation, and brokenness."[15]

Daniel acknowledges that God has righteously scattered the peoples among the nations due to their "trespass" (KJV), "unfaithfulness" (NIV), and "treachery" (NRSV). The word is *ma'al*, "trespass," used to designate "the breaking or violation of religious law as a conscious act of treachery."[16]

Note the hint of mercy in verse 9: "The Lord our God is merciful and forgiving, even though we have rebelled against him...." God's character of mercy doesn't change even though his children rebel against him. This reminds me of a New Testament passage of Paul to Timothy:

> "Here is a trustworthy saying:
> 'If we died with him,
> we will also live with him;
> if we endure,
> we will also reign with him.
> If we disown him,
> he will also disown us;
> if we are faithless,
> he will remain faithful,
> for he cannot disown himself.'" (2 Timothy 2:11-13)

God's Punishment for Israel's Sins (9:11b-14)

Daniel's prayer continues, noting the justice of God's punishment:

> "Therefore the curses and sworn judgments written in the Law of Moses, the servant of God, have been poured out on us, because we have sinned against you. You have ful-filled the words spoken against us and against our rulers by bringing upon us great disaster. Under the whole heaven nothing has ever been done like what has been done to Jerusalem. Just as it is written in the Law of Moses, all this disaster has come upon us, yet we have not sought the favor of the Lord our God by turning from our sins and

---

[15] John N. Oswalt, *bôsh*, TWOT #222b.
[16] Victor P. Hamilton, *mā'al*, TWOT #1230a.

giving attention to your truth. The Lord did not hesitate to bring the disaster upon us, for the Lord our God is righteous in everything he does; yet we have not obeyed him." (9:11b-14)

Three times in this passage (verses 12, 13, and 14) Daniel speaks of the "disaster" (NIV), "evil" (KJV), and "calamity" (NRSV) that has come upon Israel. The word is *rā'ā*, "evil, misery, distress,"[17] referring here to the utter destruction of the nation, Jerusalem, and the scattering of its people. He is referring to the curses that God promised to send upon his people if they didn't remain faithful (Deuteronomy 28:15-68). Daniel 9:13 is interesting:

"All this disaster has come upon us, yet we have not sought the favor of the Lord our God by turning from our sins and giving attention to your truth."

"Sought the favor of" (NIV), is *ḥālā*, "mollify, pacify, appease, entreat the favor of ... induce him to show favor in place of wrath and chastisement."[18] Sinners must seek the mercy of God.

What the nation has failed to do, Daniel does for it. He is not a high priest or a king or an official representative of the nation. He is a layman who has served for years as a high official in the government of Israel's conqueror. But yet he takes on this intercession. Intercessors need not be officially designated for their task. God is the one that lays the burden of prayer on them and God is the one who answers the Spirit-inspired prayers of faithful intercessors.

But I expect that others besides Daniel were also feeling the need for confession and repentance. Before the exile, love for Yahweh was sparse, but during the exile God brought about a renewal of faith. The synagogue and scribal movements began in exile and were brought back to Jerusalem with the returnees. Ezra was a godly scribe who returned to help lead the Israelites who had returned to their homeland. Probably those who felt the strongest love for Yahweh returned when they were able – the "remnant." Those who had been assimilated into the Babylonian culture and religion did not feel a need to return. Thus the exile provided a sifting and refinement of the Israelites who ultimately returned to their homeland.

A Plea for Mercy (9:15-18)

Having acknowledged Israel's sins and God's just punishment, Daniel makes his appeal. Let's analyze it so we can learn to pray prayers that God answers.

[17] G. Herbert Livingston, *rā'a'*, TWOT #2191c.
[18] BDB; cf. TWOT #656.

"Now, O Lord our God, who brought your people out of Egypt with a mighty hand and who made for yourself a name that endures to this day, we have sinned, we have done wrong. O Lord, in keeping with all your righteous acts, turn away your anger and your wrath from Jerusalem, your city, your holy hill. Our sins and the iniquities of our fathers have made Jerusalem and your people an object of scorn to all those around us." (9:15-16)

1. **God's Precedent.** God delivering Israel from Egypt provides a precedent for delivering them from Babylon (verse 15a). Neither time were they delivered for their own righteousness (Deuteronomy 9:4-5).

2. **God's Glory.** Just as God's glory was known through the deliverance from Egypt, so the deliverance from Babylon will bring him glory (verse 15b).

3. **God's Righteousness.** Deliverance of God's people shows God's righteousness as an act of mercy (verse 16a).

4. **God's Personal Identification with Jerusalem.** God has identified himself with Jerusalem, the City of God ("your city") and the temple mount ("your holy hill"). While Israel's sins have brought scorn to Jerusalem and Israel – and to God, by association – deliverance will erase that scorn (verse 16b).

    "Now, our God, hear the prayers and petitions of your servant. For your sake, O Lord, look with favor on your desolate sanctuary. Give ear, O God, and hear; open your eyes and see the desolation of the city that bears your Name. We do not make requests of you because we are righteous, but because of your great mercy." (9:17-18)

5. **Worship in God's Temple** ("your desolate sanctuary") will be filled with worshippers again. Notice that Daniel points out that this is "for your sake" (verse 17).

6. **God's Personal Identification with Jerusalem** (again). Daniel reminds God that the desolate city "bears your Name" (verse 18a).

7. **God's Mercy.** Daniel's appeal is not on the basis of Israel's righteousness, which has been destroyed by sin and rebellion. He appeals solely on the basis of God's known character of mercy (verse 18b).

A Plea for Forgiveness (9:19)

Daniel concludes with what might seem an impertinent call to action as if to hurry God.

"O Lord, listen! O Lord, forgive! O Lord, hear and act! For your sake, O my God, do not delay, because your city and your people bear your Name." (9:19)

Daniel's prayer is urgent and impassioned. But God honors Daniel's intercession for his people.

Q4. (9:15-19) What was Daniel's essential prayer? What are the various grounds of Daniel's appeal? How did God answer the prayer (see Daniel 9:20-23)?
http://www.joyfulheart.com/forums/index.php?act=ST&f=90&t=373

God did hear and answer Daniel's prayer – both by the personal messenger of the Angel Gabriel (9:20-21) and historical events that unfolded.

The Return from Exile

Daniel was 80 to 85 years old by this time and did not return to Jerusalem, so far as we know. But others did. The book of Ezra records the amazing decree of Cyrus that freed the Israelites to return.

> "The LORD, the God of heaven, has given me all the kingdoms of the earth and he has appointed me to build a temple for him at Jerusalem in Judah.

> Anyone of his people among you–may his God be with him, and let him go up to Jerusalem in Judah and build the temple of the LORD, the God of Israel, the God who is in Jerusalem. And the people of any place where survivors may now be living are to provide him with silver and gold, with goods and livestock, and with freewill offerings for the temple of God in Jerusalem." (Ezra 1:2-4)

The new Persian rulers wanted the prayers of their conquered peoples, and so cooperated with the return and rebuilding process. You can find a chronology of this period in Appendix 1 that will help you make sense out of some unfamiliar history.

What We Learn About Intercession

There are many lessons in this passage. Humility, repentance, asking for mercy, appealing to God's own interests, reputation, and glory. But the one that strikes me especially from this passage is that, as an intercessor, I cannot just pray for another. When praying for my own nation, people, or church, I must identify with their sins and confess them as mine. Taking on the sins of another as a mediator – that is the role of an intercessor, and of Christ our Lord.

Prayer

Lord Jesus, too often I take for granted what you did for us. You took on our sins – my sins. I can't do that in exactly the same way you have done it for me, but teach me to be an intercessor for my own family, church, people, and nation. Teach me to identify so that I might be a vehicle of your salvation. Teach me to intercede. In your holy name, I pray. Amen.

Key Verses

"So I turned to the Lord God and pleaded with him in prayer and petition, in fasting, and in sackcloth and ashes. I prayed to the Lord my God and confessed: 'O Lord, the great and awesome God, who keeps his covenant of love with all who love him and obey his commands, we have sinned and done wrong. We have been wicked and have rebelled; we have turned away from your commands and laws.'" (Daniel 9:3-5)

9. Nehemiah's Prayer for Success (Nehemiah 1:1-2:9)

Persian king receiving important official. The relief was once located the northern stairs of the Apadana at Persepolis (Archaeological museum, Tehran) shows a king (probably Darius the Great, 522-486). It gives you a glimpse into the pomp and power of the Persian Kings. (Photo by Marco Prins, livius.org)

It has been nearly a century since Daniel prayed his prayer of intercession. God had answered wonderfully and quickly. If Daniel prayed about 539 BC, by the next year a band of 50,000 Jews is returning to Jerusalem under Sheshbazzar (Ezra 2:64-65), laden with gifts to rebuild the temple and temple articles returned by Cyrus king of Persia. By 537/36 BC, they have begun work on the temple (Ezra 3:8). Optimism is running high. But then opposition begins (Ezra 4:4-5) and succeeds in stopping construction for the next 15 years. Not until 520 BC do they begin again (Ezra 6:13-16), completing the temple in 516 BC.[1] (See Appendix 1 for a chronology of this period.)

But then the work of restoration seems to stall once more. In the time of Nebuchadnezzar, the gates of Jerusalem had been destroyed. Whole sections of the wall around the city had been pulled down and destroyed. The city had been devastated. When the Jews returned, they had attempted to restore its defenses, but had been prevented from doing so.

---

[1] In the absence of definitive information in the Scripture, there is some dispute about when the walls were destroyed and how much was rebuilt by the early Jewish returnees. I have followed F. Charles Fensham, *The Books of Ezra and Nehemiah* (New International Commentary on the Old Testament; Eerdmans, 1982), p. 152; and Derek Kidner, *Ezra and Nehemiah: An Introduction and Commentary* (Tyndale Old Testament Commentaries; InterVarsity Press, 1979), p. 78.

A few years before we meet Nehemiah, Ezra the Priest had come to Jerusalem in 458 BC, with royal backing from Artaxerxes I (464-423), the Persian king, to restore worship and bring reforms (Ezra 7). Under his leadership the Jews had begun to restore the walls of the city and repair their foundations (Ezra 4:12).

The Samaritans and others who had gained power in the area were afraid that if Jerusalem's defenses were repaired, they could no longer threaten the Jews and would lose their power. So they wrote a deceptive and poisonous letter to Artaxerxes:

Immortal Persian guard, glazed bricks friezes found in Darius the Great's palace in Susa, now in the Louvre, Paris.

"The king should know that if this city is built and its walls are restored, no more taxes, tribute or duty will be paid, and the royal revenues will suffer. Now since we are under obligation to the palace and it is not proper for us to see the king dishonored, we are sending this message to inform the king, so that a search may be made in the archives of your predecessors. In these records you will find that this city is a rebellious city, troublesome to kings and provinces, a place of rebellion from ancient times. That is why this city was destroyed. We inform the king that if this city is built and its walls are restored, you will be left with nothing in Trans-Euphrates." (Ezra 4:13-16)

The archives were examined, Jerusalem's history of rebellion against the Babylonian kings was found, and, in the absence of a person to plead the case of the Jewish people, the king had replied: "Now issue an order to these men to stop work, so that this city will not be rebuilt until I so order" (Ezra 4:21). Jerusalem's enemies, now with royal backing, "went immediately to the Jews in Jerusalem and compelled them by force to stop" (Ezra 4:23). A local Samaritan army had crushed the Jews in the name of the king, forcing them to stop construction.

This is the sad situation that exists when the Book of Nehemiah opens. The Jews have recently lost their royal backing and their enemies are free to continue their oppression, intimidation, and dominance in Jerusalem.

Nehemiah (1:1, 11c)

> "The words of Nehemiah son of Hacaliah: In the month of Kislev in the twentieth year, while I was in the citadel of Susa... I was cupbearer to the king." (1:1, 11c)

The book begins by introducing Nehemiah, whose name means "consolation of Yahweh." The date appears to be mid-November to mid-December 446 BC. The place is "the citadel of Susa" (1:1), winter capital and palace of the Persian kings, home previously to both Daniel and Esther – 700 miles and five or six months journey from Jerusalem. Susa is one of the oldest cities in the world, going back to 5000 BC.

Though the book's author withholds the fact until verse 11 for dramatic purposes, it is important to understand Nehemiah's position: "I was cupbearer to the king" (1:11c). The cupbearer[2] is a high official in the king's household, whose basic duty it is to choose and taste the wine before presenting it to the king, to demonstrate that it was not poisoned. But the cupbearer was more than a security officer to protect against assassination. Because he had frequent access to the king's presence, some cupbearers became quite influential in matters of state, though we don't see this in Nehemiah's situation. It is likely that

Nehemiah was a eunuch, since a cupbearer would probably have had contact with the king's harem.[3]

---

[2] "Cupbearer" is *mashqeh*, "cup bearer, irrigation, drink." Used to describe the chief cup-bearer of a king, a position of trust and responsibility, also in Genesis 40 (Hermann J. Austel, *shāqā*, TWOT #2452c).

[3] Fensham, p. 157.

Jerusalem in Disgrace (1:2-3)

In verse 2, the plot thickens:

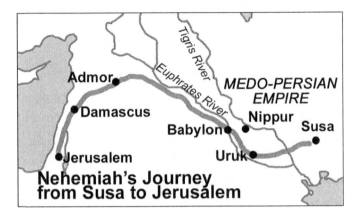

"Hanani, one of my brothers, came from Judah with some other men, and I questioned them about the Jewish remnant that survived the exile, and also about Jerusalem. They said to me, 'Those who survived the exile and are back in the province are in great trouble and disgrace. The wall of Jerusalem is broken down, and its gates have been burned with fire.'" (1:2-3)

Nehemiah's brother,[4] just back from Judah, gives him a distressing report. Apparently, the Samaritan enemies have been overzealous in following the king's command. Perhaps they not only halted construction of Jerusalem's defenses but burned the newly-built gates and demolished new attempts to repair breaches in the wall. The expedition under Ezra which had begun with such hope and promise had been thwarted and Nehemiah's countrymen are "in great trouble[5] and disgrace."[6]

Mourning and Fasting (1:4)

The effect of this news on Nehemiah is profound:

"When I heard these things, I sat down and wept. For some days I mourned and fasted and prayed before the God of heaven" (1:4)

He is deeply affected. Standing when he hears his brother's report, he sinks to the ground and sits. Then he begins to weep, bākā, "to weep, cry, shed tears." Weeping is associated with the voice, Semites do not weep quietly, but aloud.[7] He also mourns, 'ābal, "mourn, lament."[8]

---

[4] The word āh can mean, "brother, relative, fellow countryman, friend," so it is difficult to be certain of the relationship (Herbert Wolf, 'hh, TWOT #62a).

[5] "Trouble" (NIV, NRSV) and "affliction" (KJV) is rā'ā, "evil, misery, distress" (G. Herbert Livingston, TWOT #2191c).

[6] "Disgrace" (NIV), "reproach" (KJV), and "shame" (NRSV) are herpâ, "taunt of enemy, reproach cast upon another, scorn, contumely" (BDB 358; Thomas E. McComiskey, hārap, TWOT #749a).

[7] John N. Oswalt, bākā, TWOT #243.

[8] Biblical mourning for the dead involved emotion, usually expressed audibly (Jeremiah 22:18; Jeremiah 48:36) and visibly (Genesis 37:34; Psalm 35:14; Micah 1:8; J. Barton Payne, 'ābal, TWOT #6).

Weeping and mourning were accompanied by fasting (*sûm*).[9] The suffering of his countrymen in Jerusalem is his suffering. Their shame is his shame. Their exposure to danger touches a chord deep within him. Let's examine his prayer.

Great and Awesome God (1:5-6a)

> "Then I said: 'O Lᴏʀᴅ, God of heaven, the great and awesome God, who keeps his covenant of love with those who love him and obey his commands, let your ear be attentive and your eyes open to hear the prayer your servant is praying before you day and night for your servants, the people of Israel.'" (1:5-6a)

Nehemiah's terminology seems to have some similarities with Daniel's prayer of confession, which probably isn't surprising since they were part of the same Jewish community in the Persian capital of Susa:

> **Nehemiah**: "O Lᴏʀᴅ, God of heaven, the great and awesome God, who keeps his covenant of love with those who love him and obey his commands, let your ear be attentive and your eyes open to hear the prayer your servant is praying before you day and night for your servants, the people of Israel. I confess the sins we Israelites, including myself and my father's house, have committed against you. We have acted very wickedly toward you. We have not obeyed the commands, decrees and laws you gave your servant Moses." (Nehemiah 1:5-7)

> **Daniel**: "O Lord, the great and awesome God, who keeps his covenant of love with all who love him and obey his commands, we have sinned and done wrong. We have been wicked and have rebelled; we have turned away from your commands and laws." (Daniel 9:4b-5)

Nehemiah begins to pray[10] to the Lᴏʀᴅ (that is, God's revealed name, "Yahweh"), whom he describes as "the God of heaven," a phrase commonly used in the Persian empire. Like the Lord's Prayer, Nehemiah's salutation lifts his eyes to view the expansiveness of the Maker of the heavens.

The phrase, "great and awesome God" is striking. As mentioned in our study of Daniel 9:4, "awesome" (NIV, NRSV) or "terrible" (KJV) is *yārē*, "be afraid, revere,"

---

[9] *Sûm*, "fast." Fasting is depriving the body of nourishment as a sign that one is experiencing great sorrow. Mourning is further expressed in weeping and lamentation and in putting on sackcloth and ashes (Esther 4:3). He who fasts claims to afflict himself or his soul, i.e., his inner person" (John E. Hartley, *sûm*, TWOT #1890).

[10] *Pālal*, "intervene, interpose, pray," the most common OT word for prayer, which we've seen in previous lessons.

which can refer to the emotion of fear as well as to "reverence or awe."[11] We don't like the idea of a terrible or dreadful God. We would rather think of God as our buddy or "home boy." No! God is awesome. He has immense power under his sole control.

I can remember holding my firstborn son on my shoulders as I walked along the beach at Fort Bragg, California. The Pacific breakers crashed upon the shore and rocks with great noise and power. I could feel my son was almost shuddering in fear. "God made the ocean, David," I told him. Yes, God is awesome in his power. He cannot be domesticated or tamed.

He is God in all his might and power! The refrain to Rick Mullins' praise chorus has brought this phrase into our worship vocabulary:

> "Our God is an awesome God
> He reigns from heaven above
> With wisdom, power, and love
> Our God is an awesome God."[12]

Like Daniel, Nehemiah recalls God's "covenant and steadfast love" (NRSV), which the people of Israel have broken by their disobedience. Then he asks God to give him a hearing. He is about ready to go in before the most powerful monarch of his day, Artaxerxes. But first he begs a hearing from the God of heaven upon whom he depends.

Notice that this is not a single prayer, but "the prayer your servant is praying before you day and night for your servants, the people of Israel" (1:6a). This prayer is only the latest in a series of supplications that, we will see, has lasted four months.

Q1. (1:1-6) Why does Nehemiah pray day and night for four months? Why does he fast and weep? Isn't that excessive?
http://www.joyfulheart.com/forums/index.php?act=ST&f=91&t=374

Confession of Sins (1:6b-7)

Now he comes to his confession of sins, placing himself among the sinners.

> "I confess the sins we Israelites, including myself and my father's house, have committed against you. We have acted very wickedly toward you. We have not obeyed the commands, decrees and laws you gave your servant Moses." (1:6b-7)

---

[11] Andrew Bowling, *yārē'*, TWOT #907. BDB 431d, "inspire reverence, godly fear, and awe, as an attribute of God. Deuteronomy 7:21; 10:17; Nehemiah 1:5; 4:8; 9:32; Daniel 9:4.

[12] "Awesome God," words and music by Rick Mullins, ©1988 BMG Songs, Inc. (ASCAP).

We examined this aspect of prayer at length in Daniel's confession.

Reciting God's Promise to Moses (1:8-9)

But let's go on to the basis for Nehemiah's prayer. He can't appeal to God on the basis of Israel's righteousness. What is his basis of appeal?

> "Remember the instruction you gave your servant Moses, saying, 'If you are unfaithful, I will **scatter** you among the nations, but if you return to me and obey my commands, then even if your exiled people are at the farthest horizon, I will **gather** them from there and bring them to the place I have chosen as a dwelling for my Name.'" (1:8-9)

These verses feature two common verbs: "to scatter" and "to gather."

The first verb, "scatter" (*pûts*), appears 64 times in the Old Testament – the scattering of an enemy's armies, the scattering of sheep, and most frequently of God scattering Israel (Leviticus 26:33; Deuteronomy 4:27; 28:64; 1 Kings 9:6). Hamilton observes, "It is not the Assyrians or Babylonians who scatter the people of God. They are simply instrumental. God himself is the scatterer." [13]

The second verb is "to gather," *qābats*. It is used of gathering food and of money, but most commonly of gathering people for social reasons, as an army, and for religious functions. The word is used many times for the gathering of God's people from their exile in Babylon (Ezra 1:1-4; Psalm 147:2; Jeremiah 32:37; Ezekiel 34:12-13; 36:24; Zechariah 8:7-8). [14] In the New Testament, ultimately, "gathering" refers to the gathering of the saints in the rapture (Matthew 3:12; 13:30; 24:31; 2 Thessalonians 2:1).

Now Nehemiah quotes back to God his own words and promises. He doesn't seem to have a single passage in mind, but draws his thoughts from several passages, particularly Deuteronomy 30:1-3. See the parallels between these:

The Curse of Scattering

> "Remember the instruction you gave your servant Moses, saying, 'If you are unfaithful, I will scatter (*pûts*) you among the nations....'" (Nehemiah 1:8)

> "When all these blessings and curses I have set before you come upon you and you take them to heart wherever the Lord your God disperses (*nādah*[15]) you among the nations...." (Deuteronomy 30:1)

---

[13] Victor P. Hamilton, *pûts*, TWOT #1745.

[14] Leonard J. Coppes, *qābats*, TWOT #1983.

[15] Deuteronomy 30:1 uses the verb *nādah*, "impel, drive away, banish," the action of "forcibly driving or pushing something away."

The Blessings of Obedience

"... But if you return to me and obey my commands, then even if your exiled people are at the farthest horizon...." (Nehemiah 1:9a)

"... And when you and your children return to the Lord your God and obey him with all your heart and with all your soul according to everything I command you today...." (Deuteronomy 30:2)

The Promise of Gathering

"I will gather (*qābats*) them from there and bring them to the place I have chosen as a dwelling for my Name." (Nehemiah 1:9b)

"... Then the Lord your God will restore your fortunes and have compassion on you and gather (*qābats*) you again from all the nations where he scattered (*pûts*) you." (Deuteronomy 30:3)

God has scattered as he said he would, and he has gathered, according to his promise. There has been repentance and a renewed obedience among the returnees, Nehemiah is arguing.

The Dwelling Place of Your Name (1:9b)

They have consequently been restored "to the place I have chosen as a dwelling for m Name" (1:9). But Jerusalem's walls and gates are in ruins. The people are being oppressed in God's own city. You have a stake in the future of Jerusalem, Nehemiah contends, because it is the place where your Name dwells. When Jerusalem and God's people are in disgrace, it reflects on God's Name.

The Prayer of Your Servants (1:10-11)

Nehemiah concludes his prayer by appealing to God for his servants:

"'They are your **servants** and your people, whom you redeemed by your great strength and your mighty hand. O Lord, let your ear be attentive to the prayer of this your **servant** and to the prayer of your **servants** who delight in revering your name. Give your **servant** success today by granting him favor in the presence of this man.' I was cupbearer to the king." (1:10-11)

We might look upon being a servant as a lowly position. But it could also be looked at as an honor and as a privilege. Nehemiah was a servant as cupbearer to the king of Assyria – a very high honor. In a society bound together by suzerain-vassal (king-servant) treaties, the servant had a duty towards the master, but the master also had a duty to protect the servant. It was a two-way covenant. Nehemiah makes two points about servants:

1. You redeemed your servants at great expense. (Nehemiah is probably referring to God delivering his people both from Egypt a thousand years before and from Babylon beginning in 539 BC.)

2. Your servants delight in honoring you.

Q2. (1:7-11) What is the basis of Nehemiah's appeal? How does he argue his case before God? What do we learn from this about intercession?
http://www.joyfulheart.com/forums/index.php?act=ST&f=91&t=375

Nehemiah's Two Petitions (1:11)

On the basis of God's promise to restore his people to Jerusalem, and on the basis that God's servants are now calling upon his strength for protection, Nehemiah makes two petitions:

1. "**Let your ear be attentive to the prayer** of this your servant and to the prayer of your servants who delight in revering your name."

2. Give your servant success today by **granting him favor in the presence of this man**.' I was cupbearer to the king." Listen to our petition, oh God, for Jerusalem and give me favor before the king.

The Danger of Nehemiah's Request

This second petition was no "slam-dunk." Artaxerxes' policy on Jerusalem had flip-flopped and there was no way to assess his current attitude toward Jerusalem.

In 458 BC Artaxerxes had ruled positively in favor of Ezra and given considerable money for the restoration of the temple and its sacrifices (Ezra 7:11-26). But recently, Artaxerxes' policy had turned against the Jews and Jerusalem, due to the court influence of their enemies (Ezra 4:17-23).

What Nehemiah is asking God is to give Nehemiah *so much favor* that the king will be willing to reverse himself yet again. That might be embarrassing for the king and make him look weak and inconsistent. Nehemiah was a trusted servant, granted, but he seems to be more of a personal servant in the role of cupbearer than a secretary of state.

When he makes his request of the king, if the king is angry or offended, Nehemiah could quite easily lose his job or even his life! No king wants to feel manipulated, particularly by his servants who might presume upon their position to ask for personal favors.

The situation sounds very much like the dilemma Esther found herself in this very palace some 35-40 years before. Haman, a high official in the court of the Persian king Xerxes (486-465/4 BC), and enemy of the Jews, plotted to destroy the Jewish exile community living in the land. It "just so happened" that Xerxes' queen was Esther, a Jewess, but she could come into his presence only when asked upon pain of death – and she hadn't been summoned for the past 30 days (Esther 4:11). When a decree to annihilate the Jews was enacted, Esther's uncle Mordecai appealed to her to help her people:

> "'Do not think that because you are in the king's house you alone of all the Jews will escape. For if you remain silent at this time, relief and deliverance for the Jews will arise from another place, but you and your father's family will perish. And who knows but that **you have come to royal position for such a time as this**?'
>
> Then Esther sent this reply to Mordecai: 'Go, gather together all the Jews who are in Susa, and fast for me. Do not eat or drink for three days, night or day. I and my maids will fast as you do. When this is done, I will go to the king, even though it is against the law. **And if I perish, I perish**.'" (Esther 4:13-16)

Nehemiah's risk in bringing his request before the king was considerable. But he no doubt recognized that God had elevated him to this position "for such a time as this." It is time for him to stand up and be counted with God's people. So Nehemiah prays fervently:

> "'Give your servant success **today** by granting him favor in the presence of this man.' I was cupbearer to the king." (1:11)

Today is the day he will make his request. Today he desperately needs God's help, for upon his success before the king hinges the success of God's people in far away Jerusalem.

Q3. (1:11) In what way does Daniel's situation compared to Esther's? Why does God place his people in strategic positions today in the community, in business, in the military, in government? What responsibilities do we have to God that can cause danger to our positions and our lives? Has this ever happened to you? How do you pray in situations like this?

http://www.joyfulheart.com/forums/index.php?act=ST&f=91&t=376

Nehemiah prays for two things specifically:

1. "Success" (NIV, NRSV) and "prosper" (KJV) is *tsālēah*, "prosper, succeed, be profitable," that is, "to accomplish satisfactorily what is intended" (2 Chronicles 26:5; 31:21; Joshua 1:8; Psalm 1:3; 118:25; Isaiah 55:11).[16]

2. "Favor" (NIV) and "mercy" (KJV, NRSV) is *raḥămîm*, "tender mercy, compassion." The word can refer to the seat of one's emotions or the expression of one's deep emotion.[17]

Nehemiah is praying that some kind of bond of empathy or compassion will be formed between the king and him.

In the Presence of the King (2:1-4)

Nehemiah has humbled himself before God in weeping, mourning, and fasting. He has prayed. Now four months after Nehemiah's initial receipt of the news about Jerusalem, the day has arrived. Nehemiah knows it.

> "In the month of Nisan in the twentieth year of King Artaxerxes, when wine was brought for him, I took the wine and gave it to the king. I had not been sad in his presence before; so the king asked me, 'Why does your face look so sad when you are not ill? This can be nothing but sadness of heart'" (2:1-2)

Normally, servants are expected to mask their own personal feelings as they serve the monarch. But Nehemiah does not do this – purposely. Nehemiah isn't free to initiate any conversations with the king. He is a servant. But Nehemiah's countenance prompts a question from the king which Nehemiah is free to answer. In spite of the terror he feels, he says his piece, with respect, but with a clear boldness:

> "I was very much afraid, but I said to the king, "May the king live forever! Why should my face not look sad when the city where my fathers are buried lies in ruins, and its gates have been destroyed by fire?'" (2:3)

Wow! Instead of apologizing for his sadness and covering up its causes as we so often do, he is open.

An Arrow Prayer (2:4)

This is the crucial moment. The king can dismiss him from service and banish him forever from his presence. You must admit, his openness can be construed to put some

---

[16] John E. Hartley, *tsālēah*, TWOT #1917.
[17] Leonard J. Coppes, *rāham*, TWOT #2146.

blame on the king for Jerusalem's dire situation. In fact, it resulted directly from the king's own policy.

> "The king said to me, 'What is it you want?'
> Then I prayed to the God of heaven, and I answered the king...." (2:4-5a)

The king asks what he wants, and – before he answers – Nehemiah prays an quick and silent prayer (sometimes called an "arrow prayer") to God for help. Then he answers the king.

You've prayed prayers like that. "Lord, help me! Lord, save me! Lord, give me strength!" But you may not have realized that "arrow prayers" are among the great prayers of the Bible prayed by God's servants for thousands of years when in dire straits.

It is important to observe, however, that Nehemiah's "arrow prayer" was not the extent of his prayer life, but rather the overflow. Nehemiah has agonized in prayer over this issue for days and months. The "arrow prayer" is but a continuation of Nehemiah's conversation and partnership with God about this issue. *Pālal*, the common verb for prayer is used both here and 1:4. The difference is quantitative, not qualitative.

Q4. (2:4) What danger is Nehemiah in? Why does he pray quickly and silently before he answers the king? How does this quick "arrow prayer" relate to the four months of prayer he has just finished?
http://www.joyfulheart.com/forums/index.php?act=ST&f=91&t=377

Request to Rebuild the City (2:5-6)

The king has asked what he wants. Nehemiah's answer to the king is specific and well thought out:

> "And I answered the king, 'If it pleases the king and if your servant has found favor in his sight, let him send me to the city in Judah where my fathers are buried so that I can rebuild it.'
>
> Then the king, with the queen sitting beside him, asked me, 'How long will your journey take, and when will you get back?' It pleased the king to send me; so I set a time." (2:5-6)

In the king's response, Nehemiah can sense that God has indeed given him favor. The king's concern is not whether he should go and rebuild Jerusalem, but how long he'll be gone.

Request for Protection, Letters of Introduction, and Resources (2:7-9)

But Nehemiah's prayer preparation about this matter means that he also knows what he needs from the king to have a successful outcome to his journey. Jerusalem's enemies must have a clear indication of the king's backing of Nehemiah's mission, since it signals a reversal in policy:

> "I also said to him, 'If it pleases the king, may I have letters to the governors of Trans-Euphrates, so that they will provide me safe-conduct until I arrive in Judah? And may I have a letter to Asaph, keeper of the king's forest, so he will give me timber to make beams for the gates of the citadel by the temple and for the city wall and for the residence I will occupy?' And because the gracious hand of my God was upon me, the king granted my requests. So I went to the governors of Trans-Euphrates and gave them the king's letters. The king had also sent army officers and cavalry with me." (2:7-9)

At the crucial moment, Nehemiah is afraid, but through faith in the God of heaven he overcomes his fears, states the need and makes his request of the king.

We aren't responsible for the result, only for our part. It is up to God to answer our prayer, if we have prayed well and according to God's own will and purposes. In this case, Nehemiah reports:

> "And because the gracious hand of my God was upon me, the king granted my requests" (2:8).

What Do We Learn from Nehemiah's Prayer?

When I reflect on Nehemiah's prayer, several lessons come to mind:

1. God has put on Nehemiah's heart the plight of his people. We can't solve the problems of every needy person in the world, but we are part of the solution for some. God will put some needs on our hearts. Sometimes we will feel God's sorrow and anguish for others and it may affect us deeply like it did Nehemiah – with weeping, sorrow, loss of appetite, fasting, humbling, and prayer.

2. Sometimes God sovereignly places us where we uniquely can help. He expects us to do our part where we're called.

3. As did Daniel, Nehemiah confesses the people's sins as his own.

4. Nehemiah appeals to God on the basis of his promises – in this case to restore his people to Jerusalem.

5. Nehemiah appeals to God on the basis of God's own Name and reputation.

6. Nehemiah appeals to God as a master on the basis of the needs of his servants.

7. Nehemiah prayed for four months until it was time to bring the matter to the king. We must be patient in prayer and sensitive to the Lord's leading.

8. Nehemiah prays both at length in private and in brief spurts as the crisis unfolds.

9. Nehemiah acts on the basis of his prayer, willing to put himself in personal danger in order to see God's will accomplished.

Prayer

Lord, I pray for my brothers and sisters and me, that you would be able to trust us with the needs of others. That you would help us identify them. Give us vision, faith and courage. Help us not to be timid, but bold for you as we discern your will. Raise us up as your servants in every place and in every position of influence where you need your Man or your Woman to be faithful. And let us serve you there with faithfulness and in prayer. In Jesus' name, we pray. Amen.

Key Verses

"O Lord, let your ear be attentive to the prayer of this your servant and to the prayer of your servants who delight in revering your name. Give your servant success today by granting him favor in the presence of this man." (Nehemiah 1:11)

"Then I prayed to the God of heaven, and I answered the king...." (Nehemiah 2:4b-5a)

10. Jesus' Prayer of Submission at Gethsemane (Luke 22:39-46)

To me Jesus' prayer in the Garden of Gethsemane is one of the most awesome, most revealing prayers of all. It helps me understand Jesus better and love him all the more. It is a simple prayer, but not simplistic. I find it profound. But let's begin by putting it in context.

Mount of Olives (22:39)

> "Jesus went out as usual to the Mount of Olives, and his disciples followed him." (22:39)

In the phrase translated "as usual" (NIV), "as was his custom" (NRSV), or "as he was wont" (KJV), the noun is *ethos*, "habit, usage."[1] The Greek phrase means, "according to his habit or custom." Earlier, Luke explains,

> "Each day Jesus was teaching at the temple, and each evening he went out to spend the night on the hill called the Mount of Olives" (21:37).

It was a rhythm of life that week of the Festival – days in the temple, evenings on the Mount of Olives, located across the Kidron Valley from the city.

Paul Troger (Austrian Painter, 1698-1762), "Christ comforted by an Angel" (c. 1730), oil on canvas, Museo Diocesano, Camerino.

---

[1] *Ethos*, BDAG 277.

The Brook Kidron runs along a shallow canyon on the east side of Jerusalem. Across that brook begins a mile-long ridge paralleling the eastern part of the city, a hill that rises about 150 higher than Jerusalem itself. Near the base of that hill is the traditional location of Gethsemane. Luke does not use the term Gethsemane, "olive press;" the term is found in Matthew and Mark. Instead, Luke calls it the "Mount of Olives." John calls it a *kepos*, "garden" or "orchard" (John 18:1), an olive orchard that had just leafed out a month or two before.

Notice the phrase, "his disciples followed him." The verb in Greek is *akoloutheō*, "to follow someone as a disciple, be a disciple, follow."[2] The disciples followed him when the crowds acclaimed him and when life was filled with miracles. They also accompanied him – indeed, were invited to join him – when his humanity was showing, when he faced temptation in deep turmoil and anguish. Jesus was not a loner-leader, he was a leader who allowed his disciples to be close to him – even though that openness allowed one to betray him, as followers sometimes do their leaders.

Pray that You Resist Temptation (22:40)

"On reaching the place, he said to them, 'Pray that you will not fall into temptation.' " (22:40)

Jesus gives his disciples the same advice that he himself will shortly follow: to pray in the crisis, that the temptation will not get the better of them.

The verb "pray" is the common Greek word, *proseuchomai*. The content of the prayer is expressed by a Greek verbal infinitive, *eiserchomai*, "enter," figuratively "come into something = share in something."[3] Jesus doesn't encourage them to pray that they won't be tempted. They *are* tempted. Temptation is a fact of human life that neither we nor Jesus can escape. But they pray that they won't "enter into" or give into the temptation. Disciples, how do we resist temptation? Through prayer. That's the simple but vital lesson of this passage.

Q1. (22:40-41, 45-46) Why did he ask his disciples to pray? What temptation did Jesus know they would be facing? What was the content of their prayer to be? Did they actually pray this prayer diligently? How does the Lord's Prayer word this kind of prayer? Why do you think Jesus wanted to be alone during his own prayer?
http://www.joyfulheart.com/forums/index.php?act=ST&f=92&t=378

---

[2] *Akoloutheō*, BDAG 36-37.
[3] *Eiserchomai*, BDAG 293-294, 2.

Kneeling in Prayer (22:41)

"He withdrew about a stone's throw beyond them, knelt down and prayed." (22:41)

Matthew and Mark mention that Jesus takes Peter, James, and John with him, and then moves a bit farther from them, but Luke omits this detail. Luke uses the Greek verb *apospaō*, "draw or pull away ... withdraw,"[4] and describes the distance as "a stone's throw." How far is a stone's throw? my precise mind asks. A little ways. Luke doesn't tell us exactly. The point is that Jesus is alone – within hearing distance, but alone.

His posture here is different from any other time we see Jesus. The typical Jewish prayer posture of the day was standing, with eyes open and lifted to heaven.[5] Here Jesus kneels, perhaps because to reflect his urgency and humility. The Greek expression is "to bend the knees" and is found occasionally in the NT (Acts 7:60; 9:40; 20:36; 21:5; Mark 15:19; Romans 11:4; 14:11; Ephesians 3:14; Philippians 2:10).

It is remarkable that we see Jesus in this posture only once, but that in our day kneeling is considered by some traditions preferable over standing for prayer. Our prayer posture should not be decided by tradition but by our relationship and the needs of our communication with God. If standing or walking suits the situation, then that is proper. If kneeling or bowing or lying prostrate fits, then that is appropriate. Most artistic renderings of Jesus in the Garden show him with hands folded or fingers entwined, but I doubt that it was so. I know of no Jewish precedent for folding hands in prayer, and much indication that hands would be lifted in prayer.[6] The verb for prayer in this verse is the common *proseuchomai*, "pray."

The Prayer of Submission (22:42)

The content of Jesus' prayer, no doubt heard and remembered by disciples who later fell asleep, is remarkable.

"Father, if you are willing, take this cup from me; yet not my will, but yours be done." (22:42)

The prayer has four parts:

1. Address. "Father"

2. Condition. "... if you are willing..."

---

[4] *Apospaō*, BDAG 120.

[5] Leon Morris, *The Gospel According to St. Luke* (Tyndale New Testament Commentaries; Eerdmans, 1974), p. 311. I. Howard Marshall, *Commentary on Luke* (New International Greek Testament Commentary; Eerdmans, 1978), cites Strack and Billerback II, 259-262 for examples of prayer while standing.

[6] See my article, "Lifting Hands in Worship," *Paraclete*, Winter 1986, pp. 4-8. (www.joyfulheart.com/scholar/hands.htm).

3. Petition. "Take this cup from me..."

4. Submission. "... yet not my will, but yours be done." Let's look at each part in turn.

1. Address: Father (22:42a)

> *"Father*, if you are willing, take this cup from me; yet not my will, but yours be done." (22:42)

When you can observe a person under pressure, you learn a great deal about him or her. The disciples had the privilege of observing Jesus near the breaking point of intense pressure.

Isn't it wonderful that at this point, Jesus' assured address is simply, "Father"? Mark's Gospel includes the more intimate Aramaic word, "Abba."

When you and I are desperate before someone who can change our situation, we are tempted to grovel. We employ the official language used to herald monarchs – trumpets blowing, citizens bowing:

> "Elizabeth II, by the Grace of God, of the United Kingdom of Great Britain and Northern Ireland and of Her Other Realms and Territories Queen, Head of the Commonwealth, Defender of the Faith."

But Jesus is Son of God, King of kings, Lord of lords, Only Begotten, Suffering Servant, Wonderful Counselor, Prince of Peace, Bright and Morning Star, Alpha and Omega, Lamb of God – Jesus has nothing to prove.

> "Who, being in very nature God, did not consider equality with God something to be grasped...." (Philippians 2:6-8)

When he prays, he calls him simply "Father," and invites you and me to do the same (Luke 11:12).

There is something wonderfully comforting about the immense privilege of calling God "Father." He is our Father when our whole world is awry, when we are the point of death – and beyond. He is forever Father.

2. Condition: If You Are Willing (22:42b)

> "Father, *if you are willing*, take this cup from me; yet not my will, but yours be done." (22:42)

Jesus states a condition in this desperate prayer: "If you are willing...." This is a bit different from Matthew's and Mark's accounts:

> "If it is possible...." (Matthew 26:39)
>
> "Everything is possible for you." (Mark 14:36)

But the difference is only on the surface. What the Father wills *is* possible. Jesus is asking if the Father can, in the realm of his will and purpose, create a way for Jesus to avoid the cross. Luke records the absolute condition of his prayer, "If you are willing...." The Greek word is *boulomai*, used primarily in the New Testament, as in Hellenistic Judaism, in the sense of "wishing, desiring, intending."[7]

Yes, the will of God is great and creative. We can fail and get out of the will of God, and when we surrender again, God can create a whole new future for us. But Jesus' desire is for the Father's best, for the Father's highest, for the Father's desire and intention. Only if Jesus' prayer can be answered within the scope of his Father's intention does he want it answered. Only then. Only if you are desirous, my Father.

Jesus takes time to listen. Matthew and Mark record the fact that Jesus prayed this prayer three different times on that long, long evening in Gethsemane. Three times.

We are content to bop into the throne room, toss God a contract bearing our plans, and ask for his signature. Please rubber-stamp this, God, and I won't bother you. It's just a formality anyway. How blasphemously we trifle with the Father's will! Not Jesus. He doesn't ask if the Father will *permit* it; he asks if the Father *desires* it – a huge difference. Only, Father, if you desire it, do I make this petition.

3. Petition: Take This Cup from Me (22:42c)

"Father, if you are willing, *take this cup from me*; yet not my will, but yours be done." (22:42)

This is the petition: Jesus asks the Father to remove the cup from him. The verb is Greek *paracherō*, originally "carry beside" but in the New Testament it means "take away, carry away, remove."[8] The Greek word for "cup" is *potērion*, "cup, drinking vessel," and is used in the Old Testament is an expression for destiny in both good and bad senses.[9] But especially it refers to the infliction of punishment associated with the wrath of God (Psalm 75:8; Jeremiah 25:15, 17, 28; Lamentations 4:21; Ezekiel 23:31-33; Habakkuk 2:16).[10]

"Awake, awake!
Rise up, O Jerusalem,
you who have drunk from the hand of the Lord the cup of his wrath,

---

[7] Gottlob Schrenk, "*boulomai, ktl.*," TDNT 1:629-637, especially p. 632.
[8] *Paracherō*, BDAG 772.
[9] *Potērion*, BDAG 857.
[10] So Marshall, *Luke*, p. 831; and Leonhard Goppelt, "*potērion*," TDNT 6:149-153.

you who have drained to its dregs
the goblet that makes men stagger." (Isaiah 51:17)

"This is what your Sovereign Lord says, your God, who defends his people:
'See, I have taken out of your hand the cup that made you stagger;
from that cup, the goblet of my wrath,
you will never drink again." (Isaiah 51:22)

"This is what the Lord, the God of Israel, said to me: 'Take from my hand this cup filled with the wine of my wrath and make all the nations to whom I send you drink it.' " (Jeremiah 25:15)

"Jesus said to [James and John], 'Can you drink the cup I am going to drink?'
'We can,' they answered.
Jesus said to them, 'You will indeed drink from my cup, but to sit at my right or left is not for me to grant.' " (Matthew 20:22-23)

"Jesus commanded Peter, 'Put your sword away! Shall I not drink the cup the Father has given me?' " (John 18:11)

Jesus has a mission, a destiny. On earth, Jesus wasn't all knowing. This was part of the glory of divinity that he had voluntarily laid aside for a time (Philippians 2:7) when he "emptied" himself (Greek *kenoō*). As a baby, of course, he did not know all things; he learned them (Luke 2:52). As a boy he began to comprehend. In his teen years he knew more (Luke 2:49). And as he prepared for his ministry before and after his baptism, and then in the desert, the Father revealed to him the full scope of the "cup" that he would drink, the destiny to which he was called, the mission he was sent to accomplish. The scriptures spoke to him as his Father interpreted them to him.

The Destiny of the Sin-Bearer

As Jesus reads Isaiah 53 in synagogue school, he begins to understand. He is not just a teacher, an expounder of truth. He is the Redeemer.

"Surely he took up our infirmities and carried our sorrows,
yet we considered him stricken by God, smitten by him, and afflicted.
But he was pierced for our transgressions, he was crushed for our iniquities;
the punishment that brought us peace was upon him, and by his wounds we are healed.
We all, like sheep, have gone astray,
each of us has turned to his own way; and the Lord has laid on him
the iniquity of us all....
He poured out his life unto death,
and was numbered with the transgressors.

> For he bore the sin of many,
> and made intercession for the transgressors." (Isaiah 53:4-6, 12)

He is the Sacrifice itself. He is the Lamb of God who takes away the sin of the world (John 1:29). He doesn't come to be served, but to serve, and to give his life as a ransom for many (Mark 10:45). He is the sin-bearer for the people. He is the righteous one who dies for the sins of the unrighteous to bring them to God (1 Peter 3:18).

But the destiny of the sin-bearer is utter desecration as the gross and despicable sins of mankind begin to weigh upon him with an unbearable weight of filth before the Lord – lust and hatred, greed and deceit, theft and blithe promiscuity, anger and murder, selfishness and betrayal. Sins that deserve death, iniquities that inevitably drive their perpetrators into the lake of fire prepared for the devil and his angels (Revelation 20:14-15; 21:8; Matthew 25:41).

In the Garden he can almost feel what it will be like tomorrow when the sheer weight of the sins of his people literally crush him and snuff out his life.

And what of his blessed communion with his Father? How can that continue while he becomes fatally infected with sin, and sins, and innumerable sins of billions and billions of his kind who had inhabited and do inhabit and will inhabit this globe? What of sweet fellowship and trust? Of prayer and joy in his Father? There is no fellowship with sin or the sin-bearer. No wonder that he in agony shouts out on the cross the cry of desolation that begins Psalm 22:

> "My God, my God, why have you utterly forsaken me!" (Mark 15:34)

I do not know, nor can you, what this means. We have felt pain and agony perhaps, and might imagine what it might be like to be tortured to death until we suffocate upright, too weak to lift our bodies to take another breath. But the crushing load of sin? How can we understand? We cannot.

Is Jesus' plea to the Father one of weakness? Perhaps. But perhaps not. Perhaps it is a prayer to spare the Father what it will cost him, too. We can imagine the pain to the Son, but can we imagine the pain to the Father? Can we imagine how the very unity of the Trinity is threatened by the cross? Can we imagine the tension of love stretched to its very limits in putting to death the Son for sin? We cannot. Does Jesus pray this prayer to spare the Father the pain of separation? Perhaps. We cannot know.

> *But we do know* that "For God so loved the world that he gave his only begotten Son, that whosoever believes in him shall not perish, but have everlasting life" (John 3:16).
>
> *We do know* that Jesus, "for the joy set before him endured the cross, scorning its shame, and sat down at the right hand of the throne of God" (Hebrews 12:2).

We do know that Christ Jesus,

"Who, being in very nature God,

did not consider equality with God something to be grasped,

but made himself nothing,

taking the very nature of a servant, being made in human likeness.

And being found in appearance as a man, he humbled himself

and became obedient to death –

even death on a cross!" (Philippians 2:6-8)

His cup was the drunk down to the very dregs, to take on himself the wrath of God that we deserve for our sin.

Can we fault him for praying, "Take this cup from me"?

Q2. (22:42) Why did Jesus pray that the Father take the cup from him? According to Mark and Matthew, Jesus repeated this prayer three times. Why was he so intense about it? What did this mean? Why was Jesus resisting the Father's will? Or was he?

http://www.joyfulheart.com/forums/index.php?act=ST&f=92&t=379

4. Submission: Not My Will but Yours (22:42d)

And now he prays the fourth part of this prayer of desperation:

"Father, if you are willing, take this cup from me; *yet not my will, but yours be done."* (22:42)

He prays, "Nevertheless, not my will, but yours be done." In this last part of 12:42, the noun "will" is Greek *thelēma.* By New Testament times, the *thelō* word group means much the same as the *boulomai* word group discussed above on 22:42a. In 22:42d, *thelēma* means, "preference, will."[11] The conjunction used here is Greek *plēn.* It is part of a grammatical construction that indicates "on the one hand ... nevertheless" or "indeed ... but." It is a strong adversative.[12] In spite of Jesus' petition, this clause stands: Your will is primary, mine is secondary. Jesus yields, submits, surrenders to the Father's decision. Jesus has a preference – that the cup be removed. But he voluntarily surrenders that preference if the Father's will differs.

---

[11] Gottlob Schrenk, "*thelō, ktl.,*" TDNT 3:44-62.

[12] BDAG 826. Blass, Debrunner, and Funk, *A Greek Grammar of the NT* (University of Chicago Press, 1961), §447 (6).

Too often we make the mistake of praying surrender prayers without ever owning up to our own will in the matter. Instead of petitioning God to do any specific thing at all, we pray: "Let your will be done." That is good, but that is not real petition, and sometimes it can be a cop-out for determining how we really should pray. It is not wrong to come to God with a preference. But, following Jesus, after we have clearly stated our preference openly, it is then appropriate to pray, "yet not my will, but yours be done."

If we never surface and state – and deliberately set aside for the moment – our own preference, we run the risk of "hearing" God say what we want him to say. It is important to sort out what we want and ask for that – it is not wrong – before submitting to God's will, whatever that might be. Our will may very well be God's will. But it may not be. To discern God's will, we must state our own will and then surrender it to God – become neutral about the outcome if God were to desire some other outcome than ours. That is real surrender.

In this prayer of Jesus in Gethsemane, we have one of the foundational prayers of the entire Bible. Let us learn its lessons well.

Q3. (22:42) When Jesus prayed "not my will, but yours be done," was the Father pleased? Why is the Father not pleased when we are passive and uncaring and dispassionate in our prayers that his will be done? What is required for us to pray the prayer of submission with authenticity?
http://www.joyfulheart.com/forums/index.php?act=ST&f=92&t=380

Strengthened by an Angel (22:43)

Verses 22:43-44 don't appear in a substantial number of ancient Greek manuscripts, though most modern versions include them in the text.[13] Both verses are remarkable in

---

[13] Verses 43 and 44 are omitted by p75 Aleph^c A B T W f13 al f sys sa bopt Marcion Clement Origin. They are included by Aleph* D L X Gamma Delta Theta Psi f1 565 700 pm lat sycp bopt Justin, Irenaeus, and the Textus Receptus. The United Bible Societies text places the verses in double brackets and gives it a "C" probability (on a scale of A to D, A being highest), but includes it in the text. Bruce M. Metzger, *A Textual Commentary on the Greek New Testament* (United Bible Societies, 1971), p. 177, notes the strong external evidence for omitting the verses, but notes that "their presence in many manuscripts, some ancient, as well as their quotation by Justin, Irenaeus ... and many other Fathers, is proof of the antiquity of the account." He believes it less likely that they were deleted due to concern that they showed Jesus' human weakness, than that they were added from an early source. Marshall, *Luke*, p. 832 concludes, "on the whole, the internal evidence inclines us to accept the verses as original, but with very considerable hesitation." You

what they add to the picture of Jesus in Gethsemane beyond the story related by the Matthew and Mark.

"An angel from heaven appeared to him and strengthened him." (22:43)

Angelic help is found in various places in the Bible (1 Kings 19:5-6; Daniel 10:17-18; Isaiah 41:9-10; 42:6). Jesus is strengthened by angels after his temptation by Satan in the desert (Mark 1:13; Matthew 4:11). Here the text says that the angel "appeared to him," using the passive Greek verb *oraō*, "become visible, appear."[14] Jesus saw this angel. But the angel also assisted him, Greek *enischuō*, "cause to recover from loss of strength, strengthen."[15]

This raises a question. Is Jesus the only one who rates being strengthened by angels? How about his followers? I have no doubt that many believers have been visited and strengthened by angels at the times of their extreme struggles. We may or may not be aware of the angels. They may appear as human encouragers. Indeed, I am sure that God sends humans as well as angels to strengthen his children. All this is part of God's promise for us, "I will never leave you or forsake you" (Hebrews 13:5).

A few minutes after Jesus' prayer in the Garden, he is strongly aware of angels, for he admonishes his disciples not to resist his captors: "Do you think I cannot call on my Father, and he will at once put at my disposal more than twelve legions of angels? But how then would the Scriptures be fulfilled that say it must happen in this way?" (Matthew 26:53-54) God's answer to Jesus' prayer was not to remove the cup but to provide strength for the ordeal.[16]

Q4. (22:43) Did Jesus get "special treatment" because he was the Son of God to have angels help and strengthen him in his spiritual struggle? Do we get that help, too?
http://www.joyfulheart.com/forums/index.php?act=ST&f=92&t=381

---

can read more about the principles that undergird the disciple of textual criticism in my brief article, "Introduction to Textual Criticism" (www.joyfulheart.com/scholar/textcrit.htm).

[14] *Oraō*, BDAG 719-720.

[15] *Enischuō*, BDAG 337.

[16] Joel B. Green, *The Gospel of Luke* (New International Commentary on the New Testament; Eerdmans, 1997), p. 780.

Sweat Like Drops of Blood (22:44)

Jesus' need for strength is underscored by the degree of stress he was under, and as he received strength from the angel, he was enabled to pray even harder.

> "And being in anguish, he prayed more earnestly, and his sweat was like drops of blood falling to the ground." (22:44)

The word "anguish" translates Greek *agōnia*. Initially, the word was used similarly to *agōn*, "an athletic contest" and then, generally, as a "struggle, fight." In the New Testament, *agōnia* means "agony, anxiety."[17] The depth of that stress is matched by Jesus' earnest prayer, Greek *ektenos*, "eagerly, fervently, constantly," from the verb *ekteinō*, "stretch out, stretch forth."[18]

Luke describes Jesus as sweating profusely in this earnest contest of prayer. While instances have been cited of blood appearing in one's sweat at times of stress or terror,[19] I think it is more likely that the analogy is more with the dripping of the sweat than to its color or content. In other words: sweat was falling like drops of blood fall.[20]

Why Are You Sleeping? (22:45-46)

> "When he rose from prayer and went back to the disciples, he found them asleep, exhausted from sorrow. 'Why are you sleeping?' he asked them. 'Get up and pray so that you will not fall (*eiserchomai*) into temptation.' " (22:45-46)

Jesus has been pouring out his heart in prayer, but his disciples have fallen asleep. Why does Jesus come back to them? Matthew and Mark record that Jesus prays and then returns to his disciples three times. Why? I can't help but think that he is seeking their companionship and encouragement in his struggle. This may be too "human" for your view of the God-Man, but I think the humanness of Jesus seeks human comfort here.

Unfortunately, he does not find it in those closest to him. They have fallen asleep. Luke gives us the telling phrase, "exhausted (*koimaō*, "sleeping") from sorrow." Have you ever wept and grieved so much that you become exhausted by it? Have you ever been under such stress that you live in a state of exhaustion? They, too, are suffering

---

[17] *Agōnia*, BDAG 17.

[18] *Ekteinō*, BDAG 310.

[19] Henry Alford, *The Greek New Testament* (1849; Moody, reprinted 1958), I:648, contends that the text "like drops of blood" requires the idea "colored with blood." He cites Aristotle's reference to "bloody sweat" (*Hist. Anim.* 3, 19.) and an example of sweat of blood under circumstances of strong terror in an article by Dr. Schneider in *Casper's Hochenschrift* for 1848, cited in the *Medical Gazette* for December 1848.

[20] Green, *Luke*, p. 780. He compares this to Paul's simile of "wrestling in prayer" (Colossians 4:12).

grief, Greek *lypē*, "'grief, sorrow, pain' of mind or spirit, 'affliction.'"[21] They have heard their Leader agonizing a few steps away; they can sense his struggle and are bewildered at the same time as they are grieved by it.

But they cannot stay awake.

> "'Why are you sleeping?' he asked them. 'Get up and pray so that you will not fall into temptation'" (22:46).

Though they cannot help him that night in the Garden, they must help themselves, for they, too, are about to undergo a crisis in a few hours that in the dark of this night is unimaginable. They will see their Master arrested, spat upon, tried, convicted, sentenced, crucified, dead, and buried before night falls tomorrow. And most of them do *not* avoid the temptation that awaits them.

Jesus' words, of course, fit your situation and mine, too. Were the disciples sleeping? Yes, literally, but too often we sleep spiritually. We don't watch. We don't tarry in prayer. We don't stay spiritually alert. And we don't "arise" (Greek *anistēmi*, "stand up, get up"), as Jesus urged his disciples to do in the Garden, but are content with our spiritual sloth.

We must pray if we expect to avoid entering into temptation. And we *will* be tempted; there is no doubt about that. It seems like the days on which the temptation seems the strongest are those days when we haven't prepared ourselves in prayer. A coincidence? I think not.

Jesus *was* strengthened by prayer. He *did* resist the temptation of avoiding the cup that was so repugnant to him. He *did* the Father's will no matter the cost. If Jesus needed to pray to resist temptation, how much more do we?

As I consider the lessons of Gethsemane for us disciples, I see five that stand out clearly:

1. The way of the cross was far more costly for Jesus and his Father than we can possibly imagine.

2. It is quite appropriate to state to the Father our own will in a given situation. We can wrestle with God when something troubles us, so long as we can sincerely pray the prayer of submission along with it.

3. Even strong men and women must learn to voluntarily bend their wills to the Father's.

4. Angels can assist us when we are struggling in prayer.

---

[21] *Lypē*, BDAG 604-605.

5.   We disciples must learn to watch and pray so that we, too, may resist temptation.

Prayer

Father, the more I try to imagine what it was like that night in Gethsemane, the more I weep for you and Jesus. I weep for the love you have for me and my kind. To face what Jesus faced, to go through what he went through in order to purify and set me free is amazing. I am weak, but I seek to become strong like Jesus. Please teach me to pray earnestly that I might not enter into the temptations that constantly pester me. Make me like Jesus. And thank you that I can call you my Father. What a blessing! In Jesus' holy name, I pray. Amen.

Key Verses

"Father, if you are willing, take this cup from me; yet not my will, but yours be done." (Luke 22:42)

"Why are you sleeping?" he asked them. "Get up and pray so that you will not fall into temptation." (Luke 22:46)

11. Paul's Prayers for the Ephesian Believers (Ephesians 1:15-20; 3:14-21)

Rembrandt (and Workshop?), "Apostle Paul" (1657), Oil on canvas, 40.9" x 51.6", National Gallery of Art, Washington, DC.

Paul offers two intercessory prayers for the Ephesian believers in this amazing letter, though he was accustomed to ask God for extravagant blessings in other letters (Philippians 1:9; 4:19; Colossians 1:9-14; 1 Thessalonians 3:12; 2 Thessalonians 1:3; cf. 1 Corinthians 1:5). As you read Ephesians, he seems like he goes from prayer to praise and back again. He begins a prayer in chapter 1, then leaves it in praise of Christ. He concludes the prayer at the end of chapter 3 and caps it off with a wonderful doxology.

As I was trying to prepare a list of the great prayers of the Bible, first one then the other of these prayers was on the list, so I've decided to include them both in a two-part lesson.

These prayers are a bit intimidating. Paul uses such enthusiastic theological and spiritual language, you're almost overwhelmed. We can't pray like that ourselves – except by imitation of the Apostle's prayer. But his marvelous prayer teaches us how we are to pray for one another. No puny sentence prayer, but a grand, visionary, far reaching prayer for our brothers and sisters that begins in their spirit and ends at the right hand of Christ and with the glory of God. Dear friends, we need – I need – to pray appropriate, thoughtful, meaningful prayers for other Christians. These prayers of Paul help me do that and I trust they'll help you, too.

These prayers are complex and glorious in their descriptive detail. But because of the abundance of detail, it's hard to see the forest for the trees. So before we consider these prayers in detail, let's step back and look at the big picture. I've created a bare-bones outline of Paul's prayers – four petitions, four purposes and a doxology (at least that's one way to understand it). I realize that there are other ways to understand these prayers – and Paul certainly isn't laying out a logical sequence – he's praying his heart out.[1] But this will help you get a gist of it.

Petition	Purpose
Part 1 (1:17-19)	
1. May he may give you the Spirit of wisdom and revelation (1:17a) ⟶	**so that** (*en*) you may know him better. (1:17b)
2. May you may receive insight (1:18a) ⟶	**so that** (*eis*) you will comprehend and appreciate your hope, your inheritance, and God's power (1:18b-19)
Part 2 (3:16-21)	
3. May he strengthen your inner person by his Spirit (3:16) **that is,** may Christ dwell in your hearts through faith. (3:17a)	**so that** (*hina*) you can comprehend and experience Christ's love. (3:18-19a)
4. May you yourself be anchored in love (3:17b)	**and so that** (*hina*) you may be filled with God's fullness. (3:19b)
Doxology ⟶	**That** (dative) God may receive glory (3:20-21)

---

[1] I have outlined Paul's prayers in Ephesians with a certain logic and symmetry. But my way is only one way of looking at them. As Markus Barth (*Ephesians 1-3* (Anchor Bible 34; Doubleday, 1974, p. 368) comments: "Elements typical of the language of prayer defy a strictly logical analysis. At this point Paul's thinking follows the form of devotion and meditation rather than that of deduction, induction, careful subordination or coordination."

This tells you where Paul is going in his prayer. Notice that he prays for insight, inner strength, and love for the believers, for the purpose that they will comprehend/understand truth, know God better, and be filled to overflowing with God.

Paul is praying that they will finally "get it!" – have a breakthrough in their comprehension and understanding of what it's all about. Paul prays that their lives will be filled with God – which is another way to say "know him" and have "Christ dwell in your hearts."

These are the ultimate prayers that shepherds pray for the flock in their care, whether it is a small group, or a class, or a congregation. These are also the kinds of prayers that one Christian prays for another. Now let's look at Paul's two-part prayer in detail. First, in 1:15-19:

Remembering in Prayer with Thanksgiving (1:15-16)

Paul begins:

> "For this reason, ever since I heard about your faith in the Lord Jesus and your love for all the saints, I have not stopped giving thanks for you, remembering you in my prayers." (1:15-16)

Paul helped pioneer the church at Ephesus, but now it's been years since he's seen them. Many new people have joined the congregation, but he prays for them. He hears of the astounding faith and love of people in this church and rejoices. "I have not stopped giving thanks for you, remembering you in my prayers." He prays and rejoices. What do we learn about prayer for other believers here? Paul's prayer was:

1. **Continual.** "I have not stopped" indicates that Paul's prayer wasn't just once or twice, but a continued prayer for them day after day.[2] How sporadic we are sometimes in our prayers for fellow believers!

2. **Thankful.** Paul doesn't cease giving thanks to God for the believers. The verb is *eucharisteō* (from which we get our word "Eucharist"), "to express appreciation for benefits or blessings, give thanks, express thanks, render/return thanks."[3] Do we give thanks for people in prayer, or just take them for granted?

3. **Mindful.** Paul doesn't just pray general prayers but specific prayers for the Ephesians. The phrase translated "remembering" (NIV, cf. NRSV) or "making mention" (KJV), uses the noun *mneia*, which can be translated either as "remem-

---

[2] *Pauō*, "to cease doing something, stop oneself, cease" (BDAG 790), is in the present tense, suggesting continued action.

[3] *Eucharisteō*, BDAG 415-416.

brance, memory" (2 Timothy 1:3) or "mention." Here, probably the idea of mention in prayer and remembrance in prayer are both in view.[4] A number of times in his letters Paul combines these words – being thankful and remembering in prayer (Philippians 1:3; 1 Thessalonians 1:2; Philemon 1:4; Romans 1:9). How do we remember others? Having a list can help remind us, unless we have superbly trained memories. Who is on your prayer list? Do you remember them continually with thanksgiving to God?

Petition 1. For People to Know God Better (1:17)

Now Paul prays that a special revelation will come to them. He prays that God will take off the blinders, expand their minds, and help them to understand the hugeness of the faith.

> "I keep asking that the God of our Lord Jesus Christ, the glorious Father, may give you the Spirit of wisdom and revelation, so that you may know him better." (1:17)

Notice the two-fold way Paul describes God:

1. **"The God of our Lord Jesus Christ."** This doesn't detract from Paul's teaching about the divinity of Christ. Paul is just making the point that he prays to the God that Jesus himself revealed to us.

2. **"The glorious Father"** (NIV) or "the Father of glory" (KJV, NRSV). Elsewhere God is referred to as "the King of glory" (Psalm 24:7, 10) and "the God of glory" (Psalm 29:3; Acts 7:2). Jesus himself is called "the Lord of glory" (1 Corinthians 2:8). What does this phrase signify? That the Father is full of and surrounded with glory. I think of God revealing himself to Moses on Mt. Sinai in fire and smoke. The Shekinah glory of God is great, inexpressible light. Paul prays to "the Father of glory."

The means by which this prayer is to be answered is "the Spirit of wisdom and revelation." There is no upper or lower case in the Greek New Testament to guide us whether "Spirit" refers to the Holy Spirit or not. In the early Greek manuscripts all the words were in capital letters. The word *pneuma* here could refer to (1) the human spirit, (2) a quality of mind or soul that a person might receive or show, or (3) the Holy Spirit. In the long run it makes little difference, since Paul is probably praying for a quality or trait sent by the Holy Spirit. Notice how important "revelation" is. As Paul says:

> "We have not received the spirit of the world but the Spirit who is from God, that we may understand what God has freely given us. This is what we speak, not in words

---

[4] *Mneia*, BDAG 654.

taught us by human wisdom but in words taught by the Spirit, expressing spiritual truths in spiritual words. The man without the Spirit does not accept the things that come from the Spirit of God, for they are foolishness to him, and he cannot understand them, because they are spiritually discerned." (1 Corinthians 2:12-14)

Paul is not talking about Gnosticism, a religious trend of his era where secrets are given to initiates to enable them understand the mysteries. Instead, he is acknowledging the importance of God himself revealing things to people by his Spirit. Without revelation and insight that God might bring, we are dumb and blind, without a clue. Without this revelation who can know Him? So, Paul prays,

"... that the God of our Lord Jesus Christ ... may give you the Spirit of wisdom and revelation, so that you may know him better." (1:17)

Indeed, the purpose of this first of Paul's four petitions is "so that you may know him better" (NIV) or "come to know him" (NRSV). The Greek noun is *epignōsis*, "knowledge, recognition," in our literature limited to transcendent and moral matters.[5]

Just how do you cause a person to get to know God better? Teaching? Yes, that can help some. But for a person to "get it" takes the Holy Spirit's work. That is why the "work" of ministry is really prayer. That is why in this prison epistle of Ephesians, Paul is able to "work" in jail, and see his prayers answered in human lives opened to God.

Petition 2. A Prayer for Comprehension (1:18-19)

Paul continues in prayer with three specifics that he longs for the Ephesians to comprehend:

"I pray also that the eyes of your heart may be enlightened in order that you may know the hope to which he has called you, the riches of his glorious inheritance in the saints, and his incomparably great power for us who believe." (Ephesians 1:18-19a)

As Paul prays, I see a big, three-dimensional Valentine with eyes (and maybe eyelashes, I don't know). The big eyes on this red heart are closed. Not closed tightly, but closed. "I pray," Paul says, "that the eyes of your heart may be enlightened...." One eye begins to open a little, and then another. The big Valentine winces a bit as it gets adjusted to the light that is now starting to come in through squinted eyes. Wow, I can see things out there that I didn't even know existed. The other eye opens as Paul prays for specific aspect of revelation. The heart with closed eyes has now become an excited heart, beating wildly with joy and anticipation as it begins to see new things, and understand new truths. "I pray that the eyes of your heart may be enlightened."

---

[5] *Epignōsis*, BDAG 369.

The verb *phōtizō* means here "to make known in reference to the inner life or transcendent matters and thus enlighten, give light to, shed light upon."[6] Paul prays for enlightenment about three things. Though Philo refers to the "eyes of the mind," Paul's phrase, "the eyes of your heart," seems to be the first such reference in ancient literature.[7] This pregnant phrase is the inspiration for Paul Baloche's worship song, "Open the eyes of my heart, Lord ... I want to see you."[8]

Hope to Which He Has Called You (1:18b)

First, Paul prays that they "may know the hope to which he has called you." "Hope" (Greek *elpis*) is "the looking forward to something with some reason for confidence respecting fulfillment, hope, expectation."[9] Eager watchfulness. We can become bored, lazy, hopeless, listless. Jesus Christ is the hope of glory for us (Colossians 1:27). Jesus Christ's return is our "blessed hope" (Titus 2:13).

I have been meditating on the close relationship of faith, hope, and joy. Faith is "trust." Hope refers to a faith in what will happen in the future, "expectation." Joy is the direct result of faith and hope. Have you ever met a person without any hope or expectation? How sad. They are ready to die, want to die. They are apt to die by their own hand, even. Because they have nothing to look forward to, thus no joy, no faith in a future that God will bring.

God's people need hope, too. Some Christians have been caricatured as "so heavenly minded that they are no earthly good." Maybe so. But many Christians in our generation have not been taught about the promises of Christ's coming, of the Reign of God throughout the earth, of the blessings of heaven, of finally seeing his face (Revelation 22:4).

Many Christians have been taught to live in the here and now, but with no real expectation that God will answer prayer and intervene in miraculous ways. They are without hope.

In Paul's prayer he asserts that we are "called" to hope – summoned to it by God. He intercedes for the Ephesian believers that theirs will be an active faith, expecting answers to their prayers and ultimately to expect Christ to come.

---

[6] *Phōtizō*, BDAG 1074.

[7] Philo (25 BC-45 AD); *de Josepho* 147. Barth's list of antecedents doesn't yield "eyes of the heart" prior to Paul (Barth, p. 149, fn. 25).

[8] "Open the Eyes of My Heart," words and Music by Paul Baloche, ©1997, Integrity's Hosanna! Music.

[9] *Elpis*, BDAG 319-320.

We have been called to a future and a hope, to look forward, to anticipate, even to hasten Christ's coming in power and in glory (2 Peter 3:12). Paul prays for our hope to expand and embrace a big future, rather than shrivel in pain, bitterness, and discouragement or die in a parched desert of spiritual starvation. He prays that we might comprehend the hope of the future we have in Jesus Christ to which we have been called as brothers and sisters.

Q2. (1:18) How has your Christian "hope" changed your way of living? What is the result of Christians with only a meager or minute hope? How would you pray for hope to be borne in others?

http://www.joyfulheart.com/forums/index.php?act=ST&f=93&t=383

His Glorious Inheritance in the Saints (1:18c)

Second, Paul prays that we might know "the riches of his glorious inheritance[10] in the saints." What is an inheritance? The carefully accumulated possessions of another, set aside and preserved to pass on to one's heirs. Our is a "glorious inheritance," Paul says. An inheritance that is attended by glory, which consists of glory in his presence, which is rich beyond all comparison.

Moreover we are to see the riches[11] of his inheritance. It is not meager but abundant, overflowing, beyond counting.

We sometimes live lives of struggle and hurt, of love and of reaching out, but we fall so short. Paul prays that we will be able to comprehend that we have ahead of us a reward above all measure. A precious redemption purchased at great cost by our Brother, Jesus Christ.

Someone described GRACE as an acronym – "God's Riches At Christ's Expense." An inheritance. But more than that, it is an inheritance "in the saints." Ours is not a solo award, but one we will share forever and ever with all God's people, living and dead. Oh, don't worry, there's plenty for all. But it is shared with the family.

Sometimes we are tempted to isolate ourselves from others. We've suffered too much rejection, we tell ourselves. We have some painful "history" that makes us love-shy and so we practice our own form of hermit-Christianity. But our inheritance is "in the

---

[10] "Inheritance" is *klēronomia*, the common word for "inheritance," then "possession, property." Here it is used of our possession of "transcendent salvation," as the inheritance of God's children (BDAG 547-548).

[11] *Ploutos*, "wealth, abundance, plentiful supply" (BDAG 832).

saints," part of a corporate body. This truth is a portion of the revelation here of the nature of this inheritance.

Q3. (1:18) What is the result in prayer and faith if believers think that God is poverty-stricken? How does knowledge of a "glorious inheritance" motivate our lives? Our prayers? How can you pray for others to glimpse this inheritance?
http://www.joyfulheart.com/forums/index.php?act=ST&f=93&t=384

His Incomparably Great Power (1:18d)

First, hope. Second, inheritance. Third, Paul prays that we might know "his incomparably great power for (Greek *eis*) us who believe." The Greek word *eis* often carries a sense of motion, "into, in, toward, to" and sometimes is a marker of goals.[12] The use here could carry the idea of power directed "into us," "toward us," or "for our benefit." While it's difficult to say which it is precisely, the idea is still wonderful!

In this case, God's immeasurable power is into and unto us believers. It is "incomparably great" – a pair of Greek words. *Hyperballō* means "to attain a degree that extraordinarily exceeds a point on a scale of extent, go beyond, surpass, outdo."[13] The second word in this pair is *megethos*, "greatness, a quality of exceeding a standard of excellence."[14] Paul heaps one word upon another to impress upon us the extreme, humongous, immeasurable nature of the power. God's full horsepower at our disposal, working in us who believe.

What is this power (Greek *dynamis*), this "might, strength, force, capability."[15] Jesus said,

> "I tell you the truth: It is for your good that I am going away. Unless I go away, the Counselor will not come to you, but if I go, I will send him to you." (John 14:6-7)

And because this Counselor, the Holy Spirit, now lives inside of us, with us at the very deepest level, we will do greater things than even Jesus' miracles (John 14:12).

You see, the very same power that empowered Jesus' ministry on earth dwells *in us*. The very same power that called Lazarus to come out of the tomb lives *in you* in the

---

[12] *Eis*, BDAG 288-291.
[13] *Hyperballō*, BDAG 1032.
[14] *Megethos*, BDAG 624-625.
[15] *Dynamis*, BDAG 262-263.

presence of the Third Person of the Trinity. The power in the hands that touched blind eyes and made them see, that broke bread and fishes and fed 5,000 is *in you*.

But I don't see anything of the kind, you say. I feel powerless. Perhaps. All the more reason that you need God to reveal this truth *to you* – "his incomparably great power for us who believe." Paul goes on to describe the kind of power he means – "like (Greek *kata*, "in accordance with, just as, similar to"[16]) as his mighty strength which he (God) exerted in Christ when he raised him from the dead." Wow! Paul prays that we might experience the same magnitude of power that God exercised in the resurrection of Christ from the dead!

I don't see it, you contend. Exactly. That is why Paul is praying diligently that the eyeballs of your heart may be opened, that your blindness be cured, that your faith be broadened. And mine too. We live so far below our hope, our inheritance, our power.

> "'No eye has seen, no ear has heard, no mind has conceived what God has prepared for those who love him' – but God has revealed it to us by his Spirit" (1 Corinthians 2:9-10).

It has been my observation that some churches tend to grow Christians who believe in the God of the impossible, who are ready to pray with faith at a moment's notice. Other churches raise Christians with a much more intellectual, distant faith. They tend to doubt that God might intervene today, though they might acknowledge that he once intervened in history in Christ. Some churches are hot-houses that multiply faith, others are like root cellars designed to keep vegetables cool enough that they don't spoil, but warm enough that they don't freeze. Which is yours?

Prayer is not a thermometer to measure the level of faith, but a thermostat to increase the level of faith to its desired level. Whether you are a leader or a follower in your church, your prayers can help heat up the level of faith, expectation, and power-anticipation in your congregation. In fact, without your prayers the level of faith will be only mediocre. Faith will be only be luke-warm.

Dear friends, I want to learn how to pray like Paul, with a vision that sees what believers will be like when they are infused with hope, excited about their inheritance, and pregnant with power eager to be used on God's behalf. Teach me to pray, Lord. Teach me to live!

The Second Part of Paul's Prayer (3:14-21)

We have looked now at the first two petitions in Paul's two-part prayer for the Ephesians. By way of review, here's our simplified chart of Paul's petitions.

---

[16] *Kata*, BDAG 511-513, A5b.

Petition	Purpose
Part 1 (1:17-19)	
1. May he may give you the Spirit of wisdom and revelation (1:17a) ---→	**so that** (*en*) you may know him better. (1:17b)
2. May you may receive insight (1:18a) ---→	**so that** (*eis*) you will comprehend and appreciate your hope, your inheritance, and God's power (1:18b-19)
Part 2 (3:16-21)	
3. May he strengthen your inner person by his Spirit (3:16) **that is,** may Christ dwell in your hearts through faith. (3:17a)	**so that** (*hina*) you can comprehend and experience Christ's love. (3:18-19a)
4. May you yourself be anchored in love (3:17b)	**and so that** (*hina*) you may be filled with God's fullness. (3:19b)
Doxology ---→	**That** (dative) God may receive glory (3:20-21)

Now, after a long parenthesis for chapter 2 and part of chapter 3, he takes up his prayer again. Let's examine the second part of his prayer for the Ephesian believers:

"14 For this reason I kneel before the Father, 15 from whom his whole family in heaven and on earth derives its name. 16 I pray that out of his glorious riches he may strengthen you with power through his Spirit in your inner being, 17 so that Christ may dwell in your hearts through faith. And I pray that you, being rooted and established in love, 18may have power, together with all the saints, to grasp how wide and long and high and deep is the love of Christ, 19 and to know this love that surpasses knowledge–that you may be filled to the measure of all the fullness of God.

[20] Now to him who is able to do immeasurably more than all we ask or imagine, according to his power that is at work within us, [21] to him be glory in the church and in Christ Jesus throughout all generations, for ever and ever! Amen." (3:14-21)

Kneeling before the Father of All (3:14-15)

Paul begins this prayer with the words, "for this reason" (*charin*). Immediately previously, Paul has asserted, "In him and through faith in him we may approach God with freedom and confidence" (3:12). This leads into Paul's prayer on his knees. "For this reason I kneel before the Father[17]..." (3:14). Paul describes the Heavenly Father as "the Father from whom his whole family in heaven and on earth derives its name" (3:15). Bruce renders this, "from whom all fatherhood in heaven and earth takes its name," rendering *patria* here as "fatherhood" (from the related noun *patēr*),[18] rather than its normal translation as "people, family."[19]

Notice, Paul's prayer posture here – kneeling (also Acts 20:36; 21:5) – probably a posture of special earnestness.

Petition 3a. Strengthened in the Inner Being (3:16)

Now he begins the third petition of this prayer:

"I pray that out of his glorious riches he may strengthen you with power through his Spirit in your inner being...." (3:16)

Remember the phrase "glorious riches of his inheritance" in 1:18? Here again Paul reminds the Ephesians of the vast reservoir of wealth that God is able to draw on to answer our prayers. We think so small! We think so poor while our God is fabulously wealthy. One of my favorite promises in the Bible is found in Paul's letter to the Philippians. It contains the same phrase:

"And my God will meet all your needs according to his glorious riches in Christ Jesus." (Philippians 4:19)

One of the definite prayer lessons from Paul is to remind ourselves of the extent of God's wealth and resources so that we don't pray faithless prayers but big prayers. One of the slogans of William Carey (1761-1834), one of the first Protestant missionaries, was:

[17] The phrase "of our Lord Jesus Christ" in the KJV, parallel to 1:17, isn't found in the earliest manuscripts and is omitted in modern translations.

[18] F.F. Bruce, *The Epistles to the Colossians, to Philemon, and to the Ephesians* (New International Commentary on the New Testament; Eerdmans, 1984), p. 324-325.

[19] *Patria* can refer to "people linked over a relatively long period of time by line of descent to a common progenitor, family, clan, relationship," or specifically in this passage, "family" (BDAG 788).

"Expect great things from God. Attempt great things for God."

He definitely had a large view of God's "glorious riches."

From this wealth, Paul asks "that ... he may strengthen you with power through his Spirit in your inner being." There are two "power words" in this verse. The verb "strengthen," *krataioō*, "become strong."[20] It is used right next to the noun *dynamis*, "power, might, strength, force, capability."[21] Together the words have the effect of accentuating the degree of strength and power, "become mightily empowered."[22] As Foulkes rightly observes:

> "It is the constant assumption, or specific emphasis, of the teaching of the New Testament, that strength for the Christian life comes by the personal indwelling of the Holy Spirit. The Holy Spirit comes into the 'inner being.'"[23]

This phrase "inner being" (NIV, NRSV) or "inner man" (KJV) is made up of two words: *anthropos*, the generic noun for man, mankind, humankind, with no reflection of male gender, and the adverb of place *esō*, "inside, within."[24] See similar expressions in Romans 7:22 and 2 Corinthians 4:16, and the idea expressed in Jeremiah 31:33; Romans 2:29; and 1 Peter 3:4.

Petition 3b: Christ Dwelling in Your Hearts (3:17a)

In verse 16 Paul prays that the Ephesian believers may be strengthened in the inner being. In verse 17a he says this another way, using the word "hearts" as a synonym of this "inner being."

"... that Christ may dwell in your hearts through faith." (3:17a)

Heart (*kardia*, from which we get our word "cardiac") is commonly used in the New Testament to refer to the "center and source of the whole inner life, with its thinking, feeling, and volition."[25] The word "dwell," *katoikeō*, "live, dwell, reside, settle (down)."[26] It means "permanent habitation as opposed to sojourning, pitching a tent or an occasional visit."[27]

---

[20] *Krataioō*, BDAG 564.

[21] *Dynamis*, BDAG 262.

[22] Literal rendering in *The New Greek-English Interlinear New Testament*, by Robert K. Brown and Philip W. Comfort.

[23] Francis Foulkes, *Ephesians* (Tyndale New Testament Commentaries; Eerdmans, second edition, 1989), p. 111.

[24] *Esō*, BDAG 398.

[25] *Kardia*, BDAG 508-509.

[26] *Katoikeō*, BDAG 534.

[27] Barth, p. 370.

So what is Paul praying here for the Ephesian believers? The Spirit's inner strengthening is the same thing as Christ dwelling in their hearts; these are two ways to express the same truth.[28] He is praying that they might be strong in the Holy Spirit, that the Messiah in all his might and strength might fully empower them. The purpose statement (if there really is one with this petition) may be found in 3:19b.

Q5 (3:16-17) Why does Paul pray for strengthening of the inner man? How would we pray this prayer today? Why does he pray that Christ dwell in the believers' hearts? Isn't this already an established fact?
http://www.joyfulheart.com/forums/index.php?act=ST&f=93&t=386

Petition 4: Able to Comprehend the Fullest Extent of Love (3:17b-19a)

Next he prays about growth in love:

"And I pray that you, being rooted and established in love...." (3:17b)

Being indwelt by Christ, the believers naturally have a basic understanding of love. Paul refers to their present level of understanding as being rooted (*rhizoō*) and grounded (NIV, KJV) or established (NRSV) in love. The second verb is *themelioō*, "to provide a base for some material object or structure, lay a foundation," then figuratively, "to provide a secure basis for the inner life and its resources, establish, strengthen."[29] His prayer is, however, that they go beyond a rudimentary level.

"And I pray that you ... may have power, together with all the saints, to grasp how wide and long and high and deep is the love of Christ, and to know this love that surpasses knowledge. " (3:17-19a)

He prays for them "power to grasp," a phrase with two verbs. The first, *exischuō*, means, "to be fully capable of doing or experiencing something, be strong enough."[30] The second, *katalambanō*, involves the imagery of chasing someone and seizing them, then used figuratively, to "understand, grasp, learn about something through the process of inquiry."[31]

When I was in college, I worked hard to understand calculus. As a chemistry major I needed it, but despite my efforts, my grades in calculus over three quarters were C, C-

---

[28] So Bruce, pp. 326-327; Foulkes, p. 111; Barth, pp. 369-370.
[29] *Themelioō*, BDAG 449.
[30] *Exischuō*, BDAG 350.
[31] *Katalambanō*, BDAG 520.

minus, C- minus. I passed – barely – but I just didn't "get it." I couldn't wrap my mind around it for some reason. I ended up changing to a major in biology instead.

Love can be like that, too. Love is the basic thing, but so easily we miss it. We go on acting in our old selfish manner oblivious to the new life of Christ inside of us. Paul prays that the Ephesian believers will be able to shift into hyperdrive or warp speed (as *StarWars* would put it). To grasp that love isn't just the foundation, but also the whole thing – "how wide and long and high and deep."

Paul doesn't want their love to stop with mere dimensions; he prays a paradox – that they may "know the unknowable," literally "to know the love of Christ that surpasses knowledge" (NRSV). He employs the verb *hyperballō* that we saw in Paul's prayer in 1:19, which means, "to attain a degree that extraordinarily exceeds a point on a scale of extent, go beyond, surpass, outdo."[32] In other words, Paul is praying that they might know Christ's love to the *n*th degree.

Is he praying that they are able to understand Christ's *love for them* or that they themselves would be able to *love others*? Both, probably. Grammatically, the term "love of Christ" can be taken as either subjective genitive or objective genitive. But no doubt it begins with understanding Christ's love for us and grows from there.

Q6. (3:17-19) Why does Paul pray that the believers grasp the fullest extent of Christ's love for them? How does comprehending this love change a person's spiritual life? Is there any end to Christ's love for a person?
http://www.joyfulheart.com/forums/index.php?act=ST&f=93&t=387

Filled with the Fullness of God (3:19b)

Paul has been dealing with superlatives when he talks about knowing that which surpasses knowledge. And he has prayed for the inner person, for Christ to dwell in the heart (3:16-17). Now he prays what might be the purpose or the end of those petitions.

"... That you may be filled to the measure of all the fullness of God." (3:19b)

He doesn't want the believers to be half-filled, but filled (*plēroō*) completely. The term "fullness" (*plērōma*) suggests "sum total, fullness, even (super)abundance."[33] Paul prays

---

[32] *Hyperballō*, BDAG 1032.
[33] *Plērōma*, BDAG 829.

for the Ephesian Christians to be filled with "all the fullness of God." Robinson comments: "No prayer that has ever been framed has uttered a bolder request."[34]

The fullness (*plērōma*) of God is an important theme in Paul's letters. Though the term was used in Gnostic literature, it is much more likely that the roots of Paul's understanding of the word draw from Old Testament sources, where, according to Barth, it "... equates with concepts of the *shekina* (glorious presence), spirit or wisdom of God.... God fills his house or the earth with his presence, so that his 'fullness' resides at the chosen place and manifests itself with power...." The term *plērōma* "must mean the act by which God makes his power and presence felt." In verse 19, Barth renders the phrase, "Filled with all the fullness of God," as "May you become so perfect as to attain to the full perfection of God."[35] Yes indeed, it *is* an amazingly bold prayer for the Ephesian believers – a prayer I want to learn to pray for the people in my church and for the Church Universal.

Q7. (3:19) Have you ever prayed for a fellow believer that he or she might be "filled with all the fullness of God"? What would you be praying for with that kind of prayer? How does this prayer relate to Ephesians 5:27 and Colossians 1:28?
http://www.joyfulheart.com/forums/index.php?act=ST&f=93&t=388

Doxology: His Power at Work in Us (3:20)

Now Paul concludes his prayers – and indeed this first half of Ephesians – with a doxology, literally a "word of glory" (Greek *doxa* - "glory," *logos* - "word"). "Doxologies are short, spontaneous ascriptions of praise to God,"[36] usually having three parts: (1) the One to whom glory is given, (2) the ascription of "glory," and, in Paul's doxologies, (3) the expression "forever and ever." The New Testament includes other doxologies in Romans 16:25-27; Philippians 4:20; 1 Timothy 1:17; 1 Peter 4:11, 5:11; 2 Peter 3:18; Jude 24-25; and Revelation 1:6, to name a few. Let's examine this one:

> "Now to him who is able to do immeasurably more than all we ask or imagine, according to his power that is at work within us...." (3:20)

[34] Joseph Armitage Robinson, *St. Paul's Epistle to the Ephesians* (London, 1964), cited by Foulkes, p. 114.

[35] Barth, in "Comment VI. Head, Body, and Fullness," pp. 200-210. Barth draws on the research of G. Münderlein, "Die Erwählung durch das Pleroma –Bemerkungen zu Kol. 1, 19," *New Testament Studies* 8 (1962), 264-276. Barth also comments on the meaning of *plērōma* in pp. 367, 374.

[36] Patrick T. O'Brien, "Benediction, Blessing, Doxology, Thanksgiving," *Dictionary of Paul and His Letters* [DPL] (InterVarsity Press, 1993), p. 69.

God is the object of this doxology – "Him who is able," infinitely able! He is described as the one whose power is unlimited in his people. Consider the limitlessness of Paul's vocabulary describing God's power and capability here:

"Far more" (NRSV), "more" (NIV), and "above" (KJV) translate the first abundance word, *hyper*, "over and above, beyond, more than," "a marker of a degree beyond that of a compared scale of extent, in the sense of excelling, surpassing."[37]

"Exceeding abundantly" (KJV, cf. NRSV) and "immeasurably" (NIV) is *hyperekterissou*, "quite beyond all measure," the highest form of comparison imaginable.[38] This word is also used in 1 Thessalonians 3:10 and 5:13. Barth translates the phrase, "to outdo superabundantly."[39]

Notice that the limiting factor is not what we can ask or imagine. The limiting factor is the power (*dynamis*) that is working (*energeō*) in us. Whose power? God's power! Remember in the first prayer the eyes of our hearts were opened to "his incomparably great power," which was central to Paul's prayer in 1:19. There is no limit to God's power.

Paul has been praying – and instructing us in prayer. He is brimming to the top and running over with an awareness of the limitless power of God at work in us. And we worry about asking things of God that are too big. Shame on us! Our ability to "ask or imagine" may be limited, but not God's power.

God can and does work beyond our ability to ask. When you go in for an operation, you don't need to understand all the technology that will be used by the surgeon and the surgeon's team. You just have to believe they can get the job done and ask for the operation. It's their job to know more than you.

The God Paul serves is huge in his mind and faith. Nothing is to great to ask Him. And so in his doxology, Paul overflows in praise to the One "who is able to do immeasurably more than all we ask or imagine, according to his power that is at work within us" (3:20)

Q8. (3:20) How should verse 3:20 of the doxology energize your prayers? What happens when we limit God by our own ability to comprehend? How can we get past this failing?

http://www.joyfulheart.com/forums/index.php?act=ST&f=93&t=389

---

[37] *Hyper*, BDAG 1030-1031, B.
[38] *Hyperekterissou*, BDAG 1033.
[39] Barth, p. 375.

Doxology: Glory in the Church (3:21)

Having identified God in this effusive manner, Paul gets to the second element, the praise part of the doxology:

> "To him be glory in the church and in Christ Jesus throughout all generations, for ever and ever! Amen." (3:21)

Out of my early years of ministry comes a wonderful praise song by Hugh Mitchell based on this verse:

> "Unto Him be glory in the church,
> both now and evermore.
> Unto Him be glory in the church, both now and evermore.
> Unto Him, unto Him, unto Him, unto Him.
> Unto Him be glory in the church, both now and evermore."[40]

There are two ways to understand Paul's phrase, "glory in the church," depending on how you translate the Greek preposition *en*, either as instrumental or locative.[41] If you take it as instrumental, "by means of," the question is: How is the church to bring glory to him? By the way we live and love. By the way we preach the greatness of Christ. By our obedience. And most of all, perhaps, by our praise.

But you could also understand this phrase in a locative sense: "To him be glory in (the midst of, among) the church," where *en* means "in, on, at, within, among."[42] I'm not talking about the church (the *ekklēsia*) as a church building, a place, but as the gathered people of God in worship. It is a most wonderful thing to be in the house of God when praise overflows into a powerful sense of the presence and anointing of God. Some people think they can work this up emotionally. But this is beyond emotion. It is where all the people –surrounded by the angels of God – are one in giving praise and glorifying God as it is now and will be forever in heaven (Revelation 4-5; 7:10, 12; 15:3-5). Yes! "Unto Him be glory in the church, both now and evermore." We want the Shekinah glory of God in our midst and know that this comes as we give him glory through our worship and praise.

---

[40] "Unto Him Be Glory in the Church," words and music by Hugh Mitchell, © 1958, Singspiration Music. In *Scripture in Song, Book One: Songs of Praise* (Scripture in Song, 1979), #136.

[41] Sometimes, however, the senses seem to merge together. The first sense is: "May God be glorified by means of the church. May God be glorified by means of Christ Jesus," understanding *en* in the instrumental sense, "with, by means of" (H.E. Dana and Julius R. Mantey, *A Manual Grammar of the Greek New Testament* (Macmillan, 1927, 1955), §112. BDAG 326-330).

[42] Barth (p. 376) is startled by the order – the church mentioned before Christ. He observes: "Paul mentions the church first because he starts from the actual locus of God's praise. Then he adds a reference to the Messiah Jesus to designate the basis of that praise."

Meditate on Colossians 1:27b: "Christ in (*en*) you, the hope of glory." The context is the Gentile church, the pronoun "you" is plural – as if Paul were a Southerner saying, "Christ in y'all (you-all), the hope of glory."

However you take the preposition *en*, it is clear that Christ and his Church are together to give glory to God – the Redeemer and the Redeemed, the Bridegroom and the Bride. How long, you wonder? The answer is found in the third element of this doxology – "forever and ever." Amen! May its truth stand!

Q9. (3:21) How can God receive more glory in your local congregation? How can you help this happen?
http://www.joyfulheart.com/forums/index.php?act=ST&f=93&t=390

Prayer

Father, I am so humbled by Paul's prayer for the believers. My prayers seem so small and piddling by comparison. So self-centered or problem-centered. Please teach me in my heart to pray wonderful God-centered prayers that are not limited by the degree of my faith, but only by your own limitless power.

Lord, I've been studying some of the great prayers of the Bible. Please don't let my study be wasted in mere intellectual understanding. Build my spirit so that in the future I will pray great prayers to you with all my heart. In Jesus' name, I pray. Amen.

Key Verses

It's hard to narrow down the key verses in these rich passages:

"I pray also that the eyes of your heart may be enlightened in order that you may know the hope to which he has called you, the riches of his glorious inheritance in the saints, [19] and his incomparably great power for us who believe." (Ephesians 1:18-19a)

"I pray that out of his glorious riches he may strengthen you with power through his Spirit in your inner being, so that Christ may dwell in your hearts through faith. And I pray that you, being rooted and established in love, may have power, together with all the saints, to grasp how wide and long and high and deep is the love of Christ, and to know this love that surpasses knowledge–that you may be filled to the measure of all the fullness of God." (Ephesians 3:16-19)

"Now to him who is able to do immeasurably more than all we ask or imagine, according to his power that is at work within us, to him be glory in the church and in Christ Jesus throughout all generations, for ever and ever! Amen." (Ephesians 3:20-21)

Appendix 1: Chronology of the End of the Monarchy, Exilic, Post-Exilic, and Intertestamental Periods[1]

Events Affecting Israel	Approx. Dates	World Rulers	Bible Books
		Tiglath Pileser III (745-727 BC), King of Assyria	2 Kg, 2 Chron, Isaiah, Hosea
Fall of Samaria, end of Northern kingdom	722 BC	Shalmanezer V (727-722)	
Hezekiah (716/715-687 BC)		Sargon II (722-705)	2 Kg, 2 Chron, Isaiah, Micah
Sennacherib invades Palestine, threatens Jerusalem	701 BC	Sennacherib (705-681BC)	
Hezekiah's sickness	ca. 700 BC		
Manasseh (687-642 BC), wicked king		Esarhaddon (681-669 BC)	2 Kg, 2 Chron, Nahum
Amon (642-640 BC), assassinated by his servants		Ashurbanipal (669-ca. 627 BC), last great king of Assyria)	

[1] Based on chronologies in John N. Oswalt, "Chronology of the Old Testament," ISBE 1:673-685 and Roy A. Stewart and Robert J. Wyatt, "Intertestamental Period," ISBE 2:874-878.

Events Affecting Israel	Approx. Dates	World Rulers	Bible Books
Josiah (640-609 BC), "the boy king," a good king, brought many religious reforms, finally killed by Pharaoh Neco II		Nabopolassar (626-605 BC), first great king of Babylonia	2 Kg, 2 Chron, Ezekiel, Jeremiah Zeph, Habakkuk
Fall of Nineveh, end of Assyrian dominance, beginning of Babylonian dominance	612 BC		
Jehoiakim (609-598 BC), installed by Pharaoh Neco II)			
Battle of Carchemish, Babylonians defeat Egyptian army, end of Egyptian dominance. Daniel and others carried captive to Babylon.	605 BC		
Jehoiakin (598-597)			2 Kg, 2 Chron, Ezekiel, Jeremiah, Daniel
Jerusalem sacked, Jehoiakin deposed, first deportation	597 BC	Nebuchadrezzar II (605-562 BC, referred to in the Bible as Nebuchadnezzar), king of Babylonia	
Zedekiah (597-587 BC)			
Jerusalem destroyed, second deportation, end of Southern Kingdom	587 BC		
Third and final deportation (Jeremiah 52:28-30)	582 BC		
Jehoiachin freed from prison		Evil-Merodach (562-560)	Daniel

Events Affecting Israel	Approx. Dates	World Rulers	Bible Books
		Nabonidus (556-539 BC), as the last of the Neo-Babylonian kings	Daniel
		His son Belshazzar served as co-regent with him (c. 553-539 BC)	
Fall of Babylon	539 BC		
Daniel's Prayer of Confession	539 BC		
Cyrus' Edict	538 BC	Cyrus, King of Persia (539-530 BC)	
First return under Sheshbazzar (Ezra 1:1), about 50,000 returned	ca. 538 BC.		Ezra
Construction of the Second Temple begun (Ezra 3:8)	ca. 536/37 BC		
		Cambyses (530-522 BC)	
Temple construction resumed (Ezra 4:24)	520 BC	Darius I Hystaspes (521-486 BC)	Ezra, Haggai, Zechariah
Temple completed (Ezra 6:15)	516 BC		Ezra
Esther is Queen of Persia at Susa	ca. 470 BC	Xerxes (Ahasuerus) (486-465/4 BC)	Esther
Ezra and the second group of returnees go to Jerusalem	458 BC	Artaxerxes I, Longimanus (464-423 BC)	Ezra

Events Affecting Israel	Approx. Dates	World Rulers	Bible Books
Fortification of Jerusalem stopped (Ezra 4:7-23)	before 445 BC		Ezra
Nehemiah comes to Jerusalem and restores the walls	445 BC		Nehemiah
Malachi prophesies	420 BC	Darius II, Nothus (423-404 BC) and later Persian kings	Malachi
		Philip II of Macedon and Alexander the Great, rise of Macedonians and Greeks (359-323 BC) Ptolemy and Seleucid rule by Greeks (320-142 BC)	
Antiochus forced Hellenization, builds altar to Olympian Zeus on the temple mount		Antiochus IV Epiphanes (Syrian king) (175-168 BC)	1 Maccabees
Maccabean revolt under Judas, Jonathan, and Simon Maccabeus frees Israel and establishes monarchy	168-135 BC		1-2 Maccabees
John Hyrcanus as high priest and virtual king	134-104 BC		
Antipater, Herod the Great, etc.	63 BC and later	Roman domination begins under Pompey.[2]	

---

[2] See Flavius Josephus, *Jewish Antiquities* and *Jewish War* for more information on these periods.

Appendix 2. Participant Guide Handout Sheets

If you're working with a class or small group, feel free to duplicate the following handouts in this appendix at no additional charge. If you'd like to print 8-1/2″ x 11″ sheets, you can download the free Participant Guide handout sheets at:

www.jesuswalk.com/greatprayers/greatprayers-lesson-handouts.pdf

Discussion Questions

You'll find 4 to 5 questions for each lesson. Lesson 11 is a double lesson with 9 questions. Each question may include several sub-questions. These are designed to get group members engaged in discussion of the key points of the passage. If you're running short of time, feel free to skip questions or portions of questions.

1. The Lord's Prayer (Matthew 6:5-15)
2. Moses' Prayer for Israel in the Wilderness (Exodus 32:9-14)
3. Abraham's Prayer for Sodom (Genesis 18:16-33)
4. David's Prayer for Pardon and Confession of Sin (Psalm 51)
5. David's Prayer at the End of Life (1 Chronicles 29:9-20)
6. Hezekiah's Petitions for Deliverance and Healing (2 Kings 19:14-19; 20:1-7)
7. David's Psalm of Surrender (Psalm 139)
8. Daniel's Confession on Behalf of His People (Daniel 9:1-19)
9. Nehemiah's Prayer for Success (Nehemiah 1:1-2:9)
10. Jesus' Prayer of Submission at Gethsemane (Luke 22:39-46)
11. Paul's Prayers for the Ephesian Believers (Ephesians 1:15-23; 3:14-21)

1. The Lord's Prayer (Matthew 6:5-15)

Q1. What about our lives and words "hallows" the name of our Father? What desecrates and besmirches it? How should we "hallow" the Father when we begin to pray?

Q2. In what sense are we asking that the Father's kingdom should come? Why are we asking for the Father's will to be done here on earth? How should this prayer affect our living?

Q3. Why do we seek to be independent of asking *anyone* for help? Why do we seek to be independent of God? Why should we ask God to "give" us daily bread so long as we can earn a living for ourselves?

Q4. Why should we continually ask forgiveness? How can unforgiveness on our part block God's blessing? How can unforgiveness block God's forgiveness?

2. Moses' Intercession for Israel (Exodus 32:9-14)

Q1. Read Exodus 32:1-14. What had the people done that was so bad? How can a loving God be angry? Is God's sentence to destroy Israel and raise up a new nation through Moses justified?

Q2. What aspects of Moses' prayer of intercession should we emulate in our own prayers? Upon what logical grounds does Moses offer this bold appeal to God? What do you think it means to "pray the promises of God"? How does knowing the Bible help you get your prayers answered? How does this help our prayers be within God's will?

Q3. How can a wrong understanding of determinism and predestination keep us from the kind of gutsy prayer that Moses prayed? What do you call a belief that our prayers make no difference to God's response?

Q4. How can prayer change God's mind without conflicting with the doctrine of the Immutability of God? Can God answer a prayer for something outside of the scope of his will?

3. Abraham's Prayer for Sodom (Genesis 18:16-33)

Q1. What is the basis of Abraham's argument that God should spare Sodom? How does it relate to God's character?

Q2. How did Abraham demonstrate his humility before God? Why must boldness be tempered with humility?

Q3. Do you think Abraham's boldness pleased God? Why or why not? What might cause God to take delight in your prayers to him?

Q4. In what way does Abraham show persistence? Why is persistence necessary in prayer? Have you ever experienced "praying through"? What was it like?

4. David's Prayer for Pardon and Confession of Sin (Psalm 51)

Q1. In what way does a prayer for pardon require faith? What is that faith based on? How does a person gain the faith to pray this prayer in confidence?

Q2. In his prayer does David seek to minimize his sins? To maximize them? Why does an authentic prayer for pardon require clear, unvarnished acknowledgement of sin to be effective?

Q3. Is it possible to have a pure heart? How does God bring about a pure heart? What is our part in this?

Q4. What does it mean to have a broken heart and spirit? Why is this essential in the prayer for pardon? In what sense is this a "sacrifice"? Why do we tend to resist a "broken and contrite heart" in ourselves?

5. David's Prayer of Praise at the End of Life (1 Chronicles 29:9-20)

Q1. In what way do our prayers of praise "bless" God? What do we mere humans have that God desires in a blessing? What are prayers like, that *don't* include blessing God?

Q2. In what way does praise exalt God? Why should we exalt God? What does this exaltation do in us? What does it say about us?

Q3. Verses 11 and 12 both attribute various characteristics to God, such as glory, honor, and might. How might you begin to mention God's greatness in your own prayers? Where is this kind of praise found by example in the Lord's Prayer? What are your favorite songs that point to God's greatness?

Q4. Why is a person's attitude with regard to giving related to that person's attitude towards praise? Why does an attitude of possessiveness with regards to giving get in the way of worship? In what sense do all your possessions belong to God? What then should be your relationship to your possessions? How will these truths re-energize your giving? Your praise?

6. David's Psalm of Surrender to the Searcher (Psalm 139)

Q1. (139:7) Why do people sometimes want to flee from God? Why do people imagine that God doesn't know what they do? Have you ever felt this way?

Q2. (139:5, 10). In verses 5 and 10, how does God's hand touch the psalmist? Have you ever felt God's hand on you in a special way? Was it for your good? What was it like?

"Woven together" (NIV), "intricately woven" (NRSV), and "curiously wrought" (KJV) is *rāqam*, "variegate, weave with variegated threads, also with threads of gold and silver," "suggesting the complex patterns and colors of the weaver or embroiderer."

Q3. (139:13-16) How does an awareness of God's involvement in your prenatal development meant to encourage you? What might this mean to a young woman carrying a child? A young father-to-be? Why is such knowledge overwhelming to us?

Q4. (139:23-24) Why is this prayer of surrender to God so difficult to pray? When was the first time you prayed this kind of prayer to God? What was the result? Can a person be a genuine disciple without praying this kind of prayer?

7. Hezekiah's Petitions for Deliverance and Healing (2 Kg 19:14-19; 20:1-7)

Chronology of the Hezekiah's Life

722 BC. Fall of Samaria, end of Northern Kingdom

716 BC. Hezekiah begins sole reign

701 BC. Sennacherib invades Palestine, threatens Jerusalem

700 BC. Hezekiah's sickness

687 BC. Hezekiah dies

Q1. (19:14) What is the significance of Hezekiah spreading out the enemy's message before the Lord? What is the underlying principle illustrated here? How can we apply this principle to our own lives? What happens when we don't apply this principle?

Q2. (19:15) How do the first two sentences of Hezekiah's prayer (verse 15) correspond to the first sentence of the Lord's Prayer? How are they important to faith? How are they important to God answering the prayer?

Q3. Why is Hezekiah's healing important for his nation? How did it relate to God's promises to David?

Q4. (20:3) What is the basis on which Hezekiah asks for healing? Why is personal righteousness and holiness important in getting your prayers answered? How can unrighteousness prevent answered prayer if all gifts from God are by grace anyway?

8. Daniel's Confession on Behalf of His People (Daniel :1-19)

Daniel's Life Chronology

605 BC. Daniel Exiled to Babylon

602 BC. Entered service of Nebuchadnezzar (605-562)

553 BC. Belshazzar serves as co-regent with his father (553-539)

539 BC. Cyrus II ("the Great," 559-530 BC) of Persia captures Babylon,
      Dairus set over Babylon

539 BC. Daniel thrown into the Lion's Den for prayer

539 BC. Daniel prays Prayer of Confession for Israel

Q1. (9:1-3) What encourages Daniel to seek God for the forgiveness and restoration of Israel to its homeland? What trait on Daniel's part brings this encouragement to pass?

Q2. (9:3-4a) What is Daniel's demeanor as he prays? How does he prepare? Why is this so important in this case? In what ways might you and I prepare for intercession?

Q3. (9:5) Since Daniel is such a righteous man in his generation, why does he identify himself with the sins of his people? He didn't commitment them. How does this compare to how Jesus sought forgiveness for his people?

Q4. (9:15-19) What was Daniel's essential prayer? On what basis does Daniel make his request? How did God answer the prayer?

9. Nehemiah's Prayer for Success (Nehemiah 1:1-2:9)

Chronology of Post-Exilic Period

605 BC Daniel deported to Babylon

597 BC Jerusalem sacked, first deportation

587 BC Jerusalem destroyed, second deportation

582 BC Third and final deportation (Jeremiah 52:28-30)

539 BC Fall of Babylon to Persians, Cyrus' Edit

538 BC First return to Jerusalem

536/37 BC Temple construction begins

520 BC Temple construction resumed

516 BC Temple completed

458 BC Ezra goes to Jerusalem

445 BC Nehemiah goes to Jerusalem to repair the walls and gates

420 BC Malachi prophesies, end of the Old Testament

Q1. (1:1-6) Why does Nehemiah pray day and night for four months? Why does he fast and weep? Isn't that excessive?

Q2. (1:7-11) What is the basis of Nehemiah's appeal? How does he argue his case before God? What do we learn from this about intercession?

Q3. (1:11) Does God place his people in strategic positions today in the community, in business, in the military, in government? If so, do we have responsibilities to God that can cause danger to our positions and our lives? Has this ever happened to you? How do you pray in situations like that?

Q4. (2:4) What danger is Nehemiah in? Why does he pray quickly and silently before he answers the king? How does this quick "arrow prayer" relate to the four months of prayer he has just finished?

10. Jesus' Prayer of Submission at Gethsemane (Luke 22:39-46)

Q1. (22:40-41) Why did he ask his disciples to pray? What was the content of their prayer to be? Did they actually pray this prayer diligently? How does the Lord's Prayer word this kind of prayer? Why do you think Jesus wanted to be alone during his own prayer?

Parts of Jesus' Prayer
1. A_____. "Father"
2. C_____. "... if you are willing..."
3. P_____. "Take this cup from me..."
4. S_____. "... yet not my will, but yours be done."

Q2. (22:42) Why did Jesus pray that the Father take the cup from him? According to Mark and Matthew, Jesus repeated this prayer three times. Why was he so intense about it? What did this mean? Why was Jesus resisting the Father's will? Or was he?

Q3. (22:42) When Jesus prayed "not my will, but yours be done," was the Father pleased? Why is the Father not pleased when we are passive and uncaring and dispassionate in our prayers that his will be done? What is required for us to pray the prayer of submission with authenticity?

Q4. (22:43) Did Jesus get "special treatment" because he was the Son of God to have angels help and strengthen him in his spiritual struggle? Do we get that help, too?

Answers: 1. Address, 2. Condition, 3. Petition, 4. Submission.

11. Paul's Prayers for the Ephesian Believers (Ephesians 1:15-20; 3:14-21)

Petition		Purpose
Part 1 (1:17-19)		
1. May he may give you the Spirit of wisdom and revelation (1:17a)	⟶	**so that** (*en*) you may know him better. (1:17b)
2. May you may receive insight (1:18a)	⟶	**so that** (*eis*) you will comprehend and appreciate your hope, your inheritance, and God's power (1:18b-19)
Part 2 (3:16-21)		
3. May he strengthen your inner person by his Spirit (3:16) **that is,** may Christ dwell in your hearts through faith. (3:17a)	✕	**so that** (*hina*) you can comprehend and experience Christ's love. (3:18-19a)
4. May you yourself be anchored in love (3:17b)		**and so that** (*hina*) you may be filled with God's fullness. (3:19b)
Doxology	⟶	**That** (dative) God may receive glory (3:20-21)

Q1. (1:17-18). What do you learn from Paul's manner of prayer for the Ephesian believers? If Christians stopped praying for people to receive a revelation of God, would people come to know God on their own? Would God work in them at all? How important is this kind of prayer?

Q2. (1:18) How has your Christian "hope" changed your way of living? What is the result of Christians with only a meager or minute hope? How would you pray for hope to be borne in others?

Q3. (1:18) What is the result in prayer and faith if believers think that God is poverty-stricken? How does knowledge of a "glorious inheritance" motivate our lives? Our prayers? How can you pray for others to glimpse this inheritance?

Q4. (1:18) Why is a revelation of "his incomparably great power for us who believe" essential to a vital faith? How do you develop this faith in yourself? How do you pray for it for others?

Q5 (3:16-17) Why does Paul pray for strengthening of the inner man? How would we pray this prayer today? Why does he pray that Christ dwell in the believers' hearts? Isn't this already an established fact?

Q6. (3:17-19) Why does Paul pray that the believers grasp the fullest extent of Christ's love for them? How does comprehending this love change a person's spiritual life? Is there any end to Christ's love for a person?

Q7. (3:19) Have you ever prayed for a fellow believer that he or she might be "filled with all the fullness of God"? What would you be praying for with that kind of prayer? How does this prayer relate to Ephesians 5:27 and Colossians 1:28?

Q8. (3:20) How should verse 3:20 of the doxology energize your prayers? What happens when we limit God by our own ability to comprehend? How can we get past this failing?

Q9. (3:21) How can God receive more glory in your local congregation? How can you help this happen?

CPSIA information can be obtained
at www.ICGtesting.com
Printed in the USA
BVOW09s2318210717
489702BV00003B/42/P